HEALTHY GOURMET

NEW WAYS TO EAT WELL

COMPILED BY SUSAN TOMNAY

BayBooks

An imprint of HarperCollins*Publishers*

A BAY BOOKS PUBLICATION

Bay Books, an imprint of
HarperCollins*Publishers*
25 Ryde Road, Pymble, Sydney NSW 2073, Australia
Distributed in the United States of America by
HarperCollins Publishers
10 East 53rd Street, New York NY 10022, USA

First published in Australia in 1988
as *New Ways to Eat Well* by Bay Books
New editions published in Australia in 1992, 1993
This edition published in the USA in 1995

Copyright © Bay Books 1995

ISBN 1 86378 254 0

Photography: Ashley Barber
Styling: Michelle Gorry

Printed in China

5 4 3 2 1
99 98 97 96 95

CONTENTS

Health and Good Eating

*T*here's a quiet revolution going on in food. People, more health-conscious than ever, are eating smaller, lighter, fresher meals. More women working outside the home means less time available for preparing meals. Gone are the two or three big courses. A family meal now might consist of two or three dishes eaten together that once were considered simply as first courses or vegetable dishes, soup and salad, or soup and bread with fresh fruit and cheese after. Even when entertaining, the big lavish three course meal is out.

This change in eating habits means you can still eat what you like without forfeiting the waistline. Dieting isn't about a main meal of single lettuce leaf but, instead, a common sense approach to food and an awareness of its nutritional values. Eating should fit into your lifestyle, not dominate and inhibit it as can be the case when following a fad diet.

That's why this book is heavy on first courses and salads and rather light on meats. It's not a vegetarian cookbook, but it's a book that understands the mood of the times.

People are, in the main, still eating meat, but they're eating it less often, or in smaller quantities. The recipes in this book have been designed for healthy eating while also being interesting and fun!

Meatless main courses, often based on grains or legumes, are well represented. The dessert chapter is small, however there's a section on unusual fruits, mostly tropical, which are now available in some fruit markets. Fruit is the easiest dessert, the quickest, the healthiest, and except in the dead of winter when you crave something hot and sweet, the most delicious.

Good health depends on eating the right amount of the right kind of food, and eating a variety of food. Base your diet on complex carbohydrates in the form of grains, legumes, vegetables and fruit, eat a smaller amount of protein in the form of meat, fish, poultry, dairy foods and nuts, and an even smaller amount of fats, in the form of butter and oil. And vary your diet — if you want fried fish one night, have it, if you want cream in your soup, go right ahead. Just don't have it every night.

If you make sure that fiber-rich grains, legumes and vegetables are the mainstay of your diet, a splurge on rich, fatty food now and again isn't going to hurt. That's why these foods are included in the book. The food you eat should make you happy, not bored.

NUTRITION

In the sixties when people were just starting to think about getting healthy, the gurus of the time didn't even mention fiber. They talked about protein, mostly meat, as the most important part of the diet to maintain health and build new cells. Carbohydrates were thought of simply as energy foods.

Later research indicated that too much fat and high levels of cholesterol caused heart disease, and that fiber was an important element in our diet. So-called 'primitive' tribes who existed on grains, legumes, fruits and vegetables and showed no signs of the common illnesses that systematically kill us in the 'civilized' world were examined. Meat, which contains fat and hardly any fiber, became the bad guy.

Complex carbohydrates started looking good. Low in fats and high

in fiber, they produce energy and endurance. Athletes who previously would have eaten a large steak before a race now win on a bowl of pasta and vegetables.

But a body can't exist on carbohydrates alone. Proteins must be included in the diet too, and so should fats, but in moderation. The key to good health is variety.

FIBER

The foods listed above also supply fiber, much needed by the body for effective elimination.

PROTEIN

We get protein from meat, fish, poultry, eggs, nuts and dairy products. As much as possible eat lean meat; and trim the fat before cooking. Replace whole milk, cream, sour cream and butter with healthier and just as tasty equivalents: skim milk, low-fat yogurt and low-fat margarine.

Vegetarians should regularly eat legumes and grains together to ensure they get enough protein.

CARBOHYDRATES

We get carbohydrates from grains in the form of whole wheat bread, cereals, pasta and rice, from legumes (dried beans, peas and lentils), and from fruit and vegetables. These are all high in fiber and low in fat. Nuts are carbohydrates too, but they are high in fat.

Grains and legumes also supply protein, but they are called incomplete protein because singly, with the exception of soybeans, they do not supply all the amino

acids necessary for forming new cells. However, if grains and legumes are eaten at the same meal, the amino acids missing from one are made up by the other. That's why 'primitive' cultures which exist on rice and lentils are so healthy.

FATS

Generally we eat far too much fat. We get it from butter, other whole milk dairy foods and oil. One tablespoon of oil will supply our day's fat requirement. When using meat stock, always try to refrigerate it first. The fat can then be removed easily.

VITAMINS AND MINERALS

If we eat a variety of the foods listed above in the proportion of mainly carbohydrates, a smaller amount of protein and a minimum of fats, we'll get enough vitamins and minerals.

SALT

Cook your vegetables without salt, and only salt those foods that you just can't enjoy without it. If you eat a lot of processed and junk food, you should avoid salt altogether in your home cooking. Some vegetables, notably eggplant and zucchini, are salted and left to drain for half an hour or so before they are cooked. The salt draws out the bitter juices that these vegetables develop, especially when they are large. Rinse off the salt in cold running water and dry the vegetables with paper towels before cooking.

Rye

Rye flour

Buckwheat

Pearl barley

Pot or Scotch
barley

Rolled barley

Popping corn

Ground rice

Wild rice

Short grain
rice

Converted rice

Burghul

Wheat germ

Whole wheat
grain

Cracked whea

Millet

Grains: Energy food high in vitamins and low in fat.

Cornstarch

Cornmeal

Rice flour

Brown rice

Long grain rice

Bran

Rolled oats

GRAINS

Grains are the most important part of most of the world's cuisine. They keep more than half of the population alive. Grains contain carbohydrates and are an excellent source of dietary fiber. They are low in fat, contain no cholesterol, and are valuable suppliers of B vitamins, iron and calcium. Grains are called 'incomplete proteins', because they don't contain all the amino acids necessary to rebuild cells. Legumes also have incomplete proteins. But legumes contain the amino acids missing from grains and so when they are eaten together they form a balanced diet.

Many people don't eat grains in the form of bread or pasta or rice because they believe grains are fattening. However, it's not the grains that are heavy in calories, it's what you have with them. Butter and jam on bread, creamy sauces on pasta or fried rice, will all add pounds, but it's the fat, not the grains, that are doing it.

Oats
Coarse, medium and fine cut oats are readily available in many supermarkets and in health food shops. Rolled oats are much more common. Rolled oats are oats that have been steamed and flattened between rollers. It is used generally to make oatmeal and muesli, but can also be added to breads and biscuits.

Buckwheat
Buckwheat grows in northern Europe and is used extensively in Russia. Kasha, a kind of Russian gruel served with meat dishes, is

made from buckwheat, as are blinis, pancakes eaten with caviar.

Millet

A small grain, millet is cooked and eaten in the same way as rice, but millet absorbs much more water in cooking. Millet is the mainstay of the diet in parts of Africa where it is made into flat breads.

Rye

Rye is commonly used in Germany, Scandinavia and Russia. Its tough kernel should be cracked with a rolling pin and soaked in water before being cooked. It can be boiled until tender and then added to stews or mixed with rice.

Rye Flour

This is used to make black bread and rye crisp-breads. Bread made solely from rye flour is very heavy, so most rye breads are made from a mixture of rye and wheat flours.

Rice

Rice can be cooked in two ways: boiled in plenty of water, or cooked by the absorption method when 2 parts cold water are added to 1 part rice, brought to the boil, covered, and simmered very slowly until the water has been absorbed and the rice is tender.

Short Grain Rice

An all-purpose rice, used for risotto and in desserts. Italian arborio and Japanese rices are short grain rices.

Long Grain Rice

This is the best rice to use when you want separate grains, for salads, pilafs and as an accompaniment to curries. Basmati or Texmati are long grain rices.

Brown Rice

This is natural unpolished rice that has been hulled but has not lost its bran. It takes longer to cook than white rice but can be used in the same way.

Converted Rice

This is rice that has been steam-treated to reduce its cooking time. It is just as nutritious as ordinary rice because it is processed before it is hulled, which means it can absorb the bran's nutrients before the bran is discarded.

Ground Rice

Often used in shortbread or to make Asian milk desserts.

Rice Flour

Finer than ground rice, this is usually used in Asian dishes, but can be used as a thickener instead of cornstarch.

Wild Rice

This is not rice at all, but a seed from an aquatic grass which grows in the northern Midwest. It has a nutty taste and is often served as an accompaniment to strong-tasting meat, such as game. To cook wild rice, bring it to the boil in water, drain and cook in a little fresh water for about 30 minutes or until the grains are just beginning to open.

Bran

This is the thin, papery, outer layer of the wheat grain. It is one of the best sources of dietary fiber and can be eaten for breakfast and used in place of a little of the flour in cakes, breads and biscuits.

Wheat Germ

The heart of the wheat grain, it should be stored in the refrigerator because the oil it contains quickly goes rancid. Sprinkle it on breakfast cereals, toast it and use it as a topping of steamed vegetables or include it in meat and nut loaves.

Popping Corn

This is a special type corn which has been allowed to dry. To make popcorn, put a tablespoon of oil in a heavy pan and when it is hot add ½ cup popping corn. Cover the pan, shake from time to time and allow it to pop. When the popping stops, remove the pan from the heat and serve with melted butter and salt if you like. Be careful not to have the heat too high or the corn will burn. To avoid the calories, invest in an air-popper if you like popcorn.

Cornmeal

Used, especially the South, to make cornbread, Johnny cakes and hushpuppies. In Mexico and South America, a finer cornmeal (masa harina) is made into tortillas, while in Italy cornmeal is used to make polenta.

Cornstarch

This is the white heart of the corn kernel, ground very fine. It is usually used to thicken sauces and custards, and sometimes in biscuits and shortbread. Always mix cornstarch in a little cold liquid before adding to a hot sauce, or it will lump, terribly.

Whole Wheat Grain

This is available in health food shops. Soak it overnight in water then simmer for 2 hours or until it is tender. Eat the same way as you would boiled rice, with meat, fish or vegetables, or for breakfast, as you would porridge.

Cracked or Kibbled Wheat

This is exactly the same as whole wheat except that it has been cracked between rollers. Its nutritional value is the same as whole wheat and it can be eaten in the same way, but it takes only about 20 minutes to cook.

Burghul or Bulgar

This is cracked wheat that has been hulled and parboiled. Burghul is most commonly used in tabouleh (also tabouli or taboolie), the Lebanese salad of parsley, onion, mint, burghul and tomatoes.

Pot or Scotch Barley

This is the whole grain, with only the outer husk removed. It can be bought in some health food shops and should be soaked overnight and cooked for several hours until tender.

Pearl Barley

This is the type most easily found in grocery stores. Polished, like white rice, it doesn't need soaking, and takes about 1½ hours to cook. Use it in soup, with slow-cooked lamb dishes or as an accompaniment to meat or vegetables.

Rolled Barley

This is used to make oatmeal in the same way as rolled oats. It can also be used in muesli.

LEGUMES

Legumes, the name given to dried beans and peas, are a good source of protein and dietary fiber. Until recently, split peas and lentils were the most popular legumes eaten on a regular basis, usually in the form of soup. With the growing interest in Middle Eastern, Mexican and Indian food, legumes have become more popular and more readily available. Their biggest, and most well-known, drawback is their tendency to produce flatulence.

When legumes are eaten with grains, along with a green vegetable, they provide a completely balanced diet. So-called 'primitive' cultures have been eating like this for centuries.

Legumes will keep well for up to a year; if kept for longer than that, they will harden and become difficult to cook. Most legumes should be soaked in cold water before cooking, to clean and tenderize them. Discard any that are discolored or that float to the surface when stirred. If you're in a hurry, you can put them into a pan of cold, unsalted water, bring them to the boil and simmer for 5 minutes. Cover the pan, remove it from the heat and allow the legumes to cool before cooking them.

They should not be cooked in salted water as the salt will encourage the skins to split and the insides will harden. If you want to add salt, do so towards the end of cooking.

Adzuki Beans

Small, reddish-brown beans with a cream ridge, adzukis are very sweet, and are used to make flour for cakes and pastries in Japan. They among the most easily digestible of all dried beans and contain dietary fiber, protein and iron. Wash them thoroughly under running water, then soak in cold water for 2–3 hours before cooking. They should be simmered for 1½–2 hours by which time they should be tender enough to mash into a paste and use in Japanese and Chinese desserts.

Black-eyed Peas

Sometimes called black-eyed beans, these are small and kidney shaped, creamy in color with a black splotch. They contain vitamin B1, dietary fiber, protein, iron and potassium.

After soaking they should be simmered for 1 hour. Use in soups and casseroles or as a salad, dressed with oil, garlic and lemon juice.

Broad Beans

These include both lima and fava beans, and are pale to medium green when fresh. Dried, the color ranges from olive green to brown. They have a high water content, so their nutrients are less concentrated. They contain vitamin C, and some dietary fiber and potassium.

They should be soaked, and the water changed before cooking. Simmer for 2½ hours. Broad beans are the base for falafel, the Middle Eastern fried patties, and for this, they are not cooked, just soaked. They are then pounded and flavored with garlic, onions, cumin,

Legumes
The legume family — beans, peas
and lentils — is nature's recipe
for a healthy balanced diet.

Adzuki beans

Lima beans   Pinto beans   Har

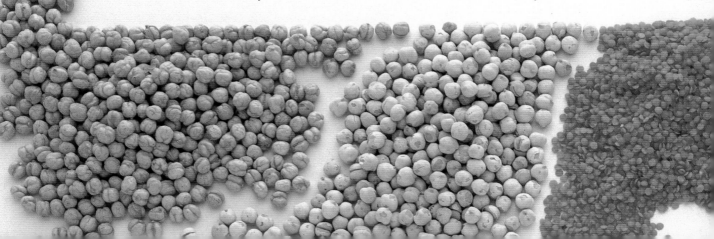

Yellow chick peas   White chick peas   Split

peas

Green mung beans

Split mung beans

Red kidney beans

Cannellini beans

Broad beans

Brown lentils

Soybeans

Cranberry beans

coriander and parsley. Broad beans are also used in soups, stews and bean salads.

Butter Beans

Similar in shape to broad beans, these are large, plump and white. They are a good source of protein, dietary fiber, potassium, vitamins B1 and B6.

After soaking they should be simmered for 2 hours until tender. Butter beans often become mushy when cooked and so they are best used in soups and purées.

Cannellini Beans

These are white kidney beans, larger than haricot beans, with squared-off ends. They are a good source of vitamins B1 and B2, protein, iron, dietary fiber and also contain calcium.

After soaking, simmer for 1½ hours. They are used in Italian dishes, particularly a salad made with canned tuna and cannellini, tossed in a garlicky vinaigrette. They can also be used in soups and casseroles. Substitute Great Northern beans or navy beans.

Chick Peas

There are two types available, the large white garbanzos and small, brown peas. Both need a long soaking and cooking time to become tender; the garbanzos less so. They contain dietary fiber, protein, iron, vitamin B1 and potassium.

After soaking, chick peas should be cooked gently for 2½ hours, or until tender. Skinned chick peas take less time — 1½–2 hours. Puréed chick peas are used in hummus, the delicious Middle

Eastern dip. In Israel they are used in falafel; in Greece whole peas are roasted in the oven and served with drinks.

Cranberry Beans

Also called borlotti beans, these are large plump kidney-shaped beans, beige to brown and speckled with burgundy markings. They are a good source of vitamin B1, dietary fiber, iron, protein and potassium. They also supply calcium and some B vitamins.

After soaking they should be simmered for 1½–2 hours. They are used in Italian dishes, particularly stews, and they are often mixed with rice.

Haricot Beans

Small, white, oval beans, these are an excellent source of dietary fiber and a good source of protein, vitamin B1, potassium and iron.

They should be boiled, after soaking, for 1½–2 hours and used to make baked beans, or stews and casseroles. They are the main ingredient in the famous French regional dish, cassoulet. Haricot beans are often used for filling pastry cases when baking 'blind'. Substitute Great Northern beans or navy beans.

Lentils

There are several types, the most commonly available are green (or brown) lentils, which can be soaked before cooking, although it's not strictly necessary, and split red lentils, which don't need to be soaked and which become tender after 20–30 minutes cooking.

Lentils are a good source of dietary fiber, protein, iron,

potassium and vitamins B1, B2, B6. Wash them thoroughly before cooking. Red lentils are cooked for 30 minutes, green or brown lentils will take 1–1½ hours. Use lentils to make soups, purées and dhal.

Lima Beans

These are very similar to butter beans and can be substituted for them. They come in two sizes, small and large. The small beans are either green or white, the large beans are white. They contain vitamin C, dietary fiber, protein, iron and some B vitamins.

After soaking, simmer for 1½ hours, but check periodically, as they may take less time. Use in salads and stews.

Mung Beans

The most common type of mung bean is the green one, but black mung beans are also available as are split mung beans. They contain dietary fiber, protein, iron and B vitamins.

They can be cooked (there's no need to soak them), but they have a tendency to become rather sticky. They are usually sprouted and used in salads and stir-fry dishes.

Pinto Beans

These are similar in appearance to cranberry beans, beige colored with brown specks. They contain vitamin B1, iron, protein, potassium, dietary fiber and some calcium.

After soaking, simmer them for 1–1½ hours and use in stews, soups, and other meat and bean dishes.

Red Kidney Beans

Dark red, kidney-shaped beans, they contain dietary fiber,

protein, iron, potassium and several B vitamins.

They should be soaked and then simmered for 1½ hours and fried with onions and chiles as a filling for tacos, in chile con carne, and in soups and casseroles.

Soybeans

These are small, very hard beige-colored oval beans. They are the most nutritious of all beans, containing vitamin B1, protein, iron, dietary fiber and calcium. The Chinese, who have been using soybeans and soybean products for thousands of years, call them 'the meat of the earth'.

They take a very long time to become tender. After soaking, cover them with fresh water and simmer for 3½–4 hours. They can be used to make very nutritious baked beans, or in any dish that requires red kidney beans or haricot beans, increasing the cooking times accordingly.

Split Peas

These are probably the most well-known legumes. Everyone at some time has had pea soup with or without ham. There are two types available, green and yellow. They are a good source of vitamin B1, protein, iron, pantothenic acid, potassium, dietary fiber and some other B vitamins.

Split peas don't need to be soaked. They should be covered with plenty of cold water and simmered for 1½ hours without stirring (stirring will encourage them to stick to the pan). Use in soups and puréed, as a vegetable.

Whole Dried Peas

These are blue-green or brown, round, dimpled and hard dry peas. Blue peas produce green split peas, brown peas produce yellow split peas. They contain vitamin B1, protein, potassium, dietary fiber, iron, pantothenic acid and other B vitamins.

They should be soaked overnight and cooked in fresh water for 1 hour. They break up during cooking so should be used in soups or as a purée.

VEGETABLES

Asparagus

The asparagus season is short so make the most of it. When buying asparagus, look for firm stalks with no wrinkling. The tips should be tightly furled and shouldn't wilt. Wash them well before cooking. Thin asparagus doesn't need to be peeled, but thick asparagus should have its stalks peeled before cooking, because it can be a bit woody.

Cut or break off the white, woody base and tie the stalks in bundles. If you have a mixture of thick and thin stalks, cook the thick stalks first, and add the thin stalks later, since they don't take as long to cook. Stand them upright in an asparagus steamer or in a saucepan with boiling water to come about a third of the way up the stems. Cover with foil, or an upturned saucepan of the same diameter, so that the stalks will boil and the tips will steam.

The most common mistake in cooking asparagus is to overcook it.

Test thin asparagus after 5 minutes, thick asparagus after 8 minutes; you should be able to pierce the stem with a skewer, but it should still be firm. Peeled asparagus takes less time to cook. Asparagus may be eaten with the fingers and is usually served hot with melted butter or hollandaise sauce and cold with vinaigrette.

Artichokes

Globe artichokes look like large thistles and should have their stalks or bases trimmed flat so they sit straight. Cut off about ¼ of the top of the artichoke, wash it and boil in water acidulated with lemon juice. Alternatively you can tie a slice of lemon to each artichoke. This prevents it from browning. Test by pulling away one of the leaves. When it comes off easily, the artichoke is cooked. Never cook artichokes in an aluminum pan, as they will discolor the pot.

To eat a whole artichoke, pull of the leaves, one at a time, and dip into melted butter or hollandaise sauce, then draw it through your teeth, eating only the fleshy part at the bottom of the leaf and discarding the rest. Cold artichokes can be dipped into vinaigrette.

At the center of the artichoke is a little cone of light-colored leaves. Pull these off and scrape out the hairy choke with a teaspoon. The heart of the artichoke, which is considered the best part, can be eaten with a knife and fork.

Chinese
cabbage

Sugar peas

Vegetables
The variety and flavor of versatile vegetables.
Great with every meal or on their own.

Snow peas

Banana chiles

Baby eggplant

Eggplant

Bok choy

Oyster
mushrooms

Fennel

Belgian endive

Artichoke

Curly
endive

Jerusalem
artichoke

Chiles

Kohlrabi

Taro

Scallions

Spinach

Jerusalem Artichokes

These are not in any way similar to globe artichokes, but are small knobby tubers. Scrub and peel and use immediately, as their flesh turns a grayish-purple when exposed to the air. Boil in acidulated water to prevent this. Once boiled they may be sautéed in oil or butter until golden brown.

Scallions

Mild-mannered members of the onion family which have a white bulb with long green tops and are sold in bunches. Use the white bulb and include a little of the green stem. Slightly larger, round bulbs are marketed as spring onions.

French Shallots

Real shallots grow in little bulbs just like garlic, but have a red, papery skin, and purplish flesh. Although not as pungent as ordinary onions, they have a more intense flavor, suitable for using in subtly-flavored sauces, such as beurre blanc.

Belgian Endive

Also called chicory or Witloof, Belgian endive consists of tightly clustered, smooth white leaves with yellow tips. It is often used raw in a salad, by itself or with other greens, sliced diagonally and dressed with oil and lemon juice. Endive is also good braised in butter, but it is slightly bitter when cooked, so first blanch it in water acidulated with a little lemon juice, then drain and braise.

Eggplant

Eggplants come in a variety of colors and sizes, from small white egg shapes, through purple striped, to large deep purple fruits. The large ones need to be salted before cooking, to eliminate their bitter juices. Slice or cut, according to your recipe, sprinkle with salt and let drain in a colander or on paper towels for 30 minutes. Don't peel. Rinse well and dry with paper towels. Baby eggplants usually don't require salting. If you're frying eggplants, use good quality olive oil for the most delicious combination of flavors.

Curly Endive

A salad vegetable with curly leaves, this is also known as chicory. Make it into a salad in exactly the same way you would lettuce, i.e., wash it and drain it well. Because endive is more bitter than lettuce, it needs a strongly-flavored dressing, perhaps made with mustard or blue cheese, and it goes well with such additions as crumbled grilled bacon, anchovies and olives.

Spinach

There are two types. The light green, smooth-leafed spinach is generally seen in the summer months; the dark green, thicker curly-leafed is normally available in the winter. However it wilts very quickly and should be bought and used when it's fresh. Spinach is delicious in salads, or as a hot vegetable.

For winter spinach, the stalks and midribs should be removed from each leaf if they are coarse. This is done by folding the spinach leaf inwards and pulling the stalk up towards the tip.

Wash the leaves very thoroughly in a few changes of water as spinach can be very sandy, and, if to be served hot, cook in just the water that clings to it. When wilted, it is drained thoroughly, chopped finely and mixed with pepper, a little freshly grated nutmeg, some butter or cream.

Watercress

Watercress make delicious soups, sauces and sandwiches; it is also used as a garnish. The most boring thing about watercress is that to use it in any edible form — not simply as a garnish — the leaves must be pulled off the stems. This can take some time. It has a slightly peppery taste and is an excellent addition to a green salad that would otherwise be bland.

Chinese Cabbage

An elongated white head with green edged leaves, this is used in the same way as you would ordinary cabbage, but it is most often used in Chinese dishes. It is delicious braised with oyster sauce. Not to be confused with bok choy.

Bok Choy

This grows in bunches with white fleshy stems and olive green leaves. You can buy it in most Asian stores that sell fresh vegetables, and it is now becoming more readily available at traditional greengrocers.

The tough stalk ends are discarded, but the stalks themselves are sliced and used with the leaves. It is mostly used in Chinese stir-fry recipes. Do not overcook, or the texture will be ruined.

Kohlrabi

The edible part of the kohlrabi is its

bulbous stem. It has shoots growing out of the bulb, which should be cut off when preparing it for cooking. Choose the smallest kohlrabi you can find — the vegetable becomes coarse and fibrous as it grows larger. Peel, cut off the shoots and cook, whole or sliced, in boiling water. They can then be sliced into julienne strips, tossed in vinaigrette and eaten as a salad, or sautéed in butter for a few minutes. Kohlrabi has a delicate turnip flavor.

Mushrooms

Mushroom varieties are sprouting like, well, mushrooms. Oysters, pleurettes, shitakes, portobellos, and even porcinis are now available as alternatives to the standard, white buttons. They should be clean and fresh looking, with no sign of sliminess. Brush off any compost (don't rinse) and trim stalk end. They can be eaten raw, or sautéed or even broiled.

Snow Peas

Snow peas need to be trimmed and strung. To do this, break off the tip at one end and pull it down, removing the string as you go. Break off the tip at the other end, and pull it up, taking off the string on the other side. If boiled or steamed whole for a few minutes only, they should remain crisp. Snow peas can be cut into julienne strips and blanched for 1–2 minutes, then refreshed in cold water, drained and added to salads.

Chiles

There are more than one hundred types of chiles, many of which are now available at greenmarkets or in gourmet shops. Color is not an indication of heat, nor is size. It's best to check before you buy. If you want the taste of chiles in a dish, but not the searing hotness, remove the seeds. When working with hot chiles, wear rubber gloves, and don't rub your face or eyes until the gloves are off!

Banana Chiles

Similar to Hungarian chiles, but smaller. On a scale of 1 to 10, these would rate about a 2.

Fennel

Fennel tastes of anise, and is either loved or hated. Buy it as fresh as possible. It should be white with a greenish tinge and the feathery leaves on top should look fresh. Any sign of yellow is a sign of age. Fennel can be chopped and eaten as a salad with vinaigrette, added to a mixed salad or braised in butter or oil.

The leaves should be cut off, and the base should be trimmed. Then the fennel can be cut across into rings or vertically into leaves.

Sugar Peas (Snap Peas)

These have only been available for a few years and are quickly becoming popular. They are very sweet and the whole pea including the pod is eaten, just like snow peas. They should be trimmed, and cooked quickly in salted water. They can be eaten cold in salads or hot, just as you would ordinary peas.

Okra

Okra is a slightly furry vegetable, which, when cut, secretes a ropy liquid. This viscous texture gives body to the stews in which they are often used. Creole and Cajun gumbos are the most famous dishes to include okra. Look for crisp, small pods, discarding any that are shriveled. To cook them, scrub well, and preferably cook whole. If trimmed, try not to expose the seeds or the okra will split during cooking and lose its shape.

Taro

In the photograph we have shown two types of taro which are available. They are not often seen in shops, but are becoming more popular and can be treated in much the same way as potatoes. They should be peeled, then boiled and mashed, or baked or sautéed. When boiled, the flesh will turn a grayish-green color.

FRUITS

A platter piled high with fresh fruits is undoubtedly one of the most refreshing, delicious and simple ways to end a meal.

With people becoming more and more health conscious, fruit is a definite asset in this food revolution of changing eating patterns. Most of the desserts in this book consist of fresh, as well as some dried, fruits prepared and presented in interesting ways.

Full of minerals and vitamins, fresh fruit is great for snacks, as the base for appetizers, soups, main meals plus its more traditional role in jams, chutneys and drinks. Its versatility extends beyond use in cooking though. Contents scooped out of fruits such as grapefruit, melon, oranges, pineapples and avocados leave shells which make novel serving dishes.

Pomegranate

Lim

Tangelo

Raspberries

Dates

Kiwifruit

Blueberries

Cherries

Red
papaya

Lychees

Red currants

Fruits
For snacks, starters and great
endings, delicious, nutritious
fruit is the answer.

Christmas
apples

Plums

Rambutan

Blackberries

ango

Loquats

Coconut

Peach

Papaya leaves wrapped around meat or octopus overnight, or papaya juice poured over meats, are ideal as natural tenderizers.

Blueberry

These little black or dull blue colored fruits grow in clusters on shrubs. They are used in muffins, pancakes, pies, cakes and biscuits, in sauces and stewed either alone or with apples, pears and quince. Blueberries go very well with spices such as cinnamon, coriander, ginger, nutmeg and cardamom. Serve fresh with sour cream or cottage cheese and brown sugar.

Raspberries

Raspberries are one of the sweetest and most delectable of berries. Raspberries can be eaten fresh, or served in compotes, cakes, flans, tarts, pancakes, jams or jellies. Raspberries puréed with cream are a tasty dressing for fruit desserts.

Tangelo

Juicy and good for eating or use in salads, the tangelo is a hybrid fruit; that is, a cross between a orange and a grapefruit. Tangelos are easy to peel and to section.

Avocado

Highly nutritional and easy to digest, avocados are available year round. There are over 70 different varieties with the three most popular ones being the smooth green Sharwil, the pebbled Fuerte and the slightly smaller purplish-black Hass. They are soft but firm when ripe. Avocado is the basis of the delicious Mexican dip, guacamole. Sliced avocado is popular in salads and puréed

avocado combined with other ingredients makes tasty sauces. Lemon juice sprinkled over avocado slices prevents browning. If cooking with avocado, its delicate, subtle flavors can easily be destroyed if overheated.

Blackberry

Blackberries are very nourishing, containing a high proportion of calcium and vitamin B1, plus other vitamins and minerals. The fruit is first green and as it ripens turns red and then a deep black. Blackberries can be served fresh or else in jams, tarts, etc. Because of their 'pippy' texture, a lot of blackberry cooking requires straining the pulp and using the extracted juice.

Lychees

When ripe, the skin of the lychee should be red. They taste best when they're slightly chilled. Peel and eat them just as they are, removing the glossy pit in the center. Lychees are also good mixed with strawberries, mandarin oranges, or other fruit.

Mangoes

Avoid buying mangoes with black marks on the skin; they indicate that rot might be present. Mangoes are extremely messy to eat; most experts agree that to eat a mango whole, one should do it in the bath. To serve a mango elegantly, cut it down both sides of the seed, to give two fat 'cheeks'. Score the mango flesh diagonally with a sharp knife, then turn and score it diagonally the other way, to make a diamond pattern. Make sure you don't cut right through to the skin. Holding the mango at both corners,

turn it outwards so that the little diamonds pop up. Serve with a spoon and fork. That leaves you with the mango pit and all the flesh adhering to it. You have little choice but to suck it over the kitchen sink.

Rambutan

Treatment of this odd looking fruit is very similar to that of lychees — peel it, eat the flesh and discard the seed. The flesh can be eaten fresh, used in salads, canned, preserved or bottled. Originating from Malaysia, rambutan flesh is white to gray and adheres to a flattened seed.

Red Currants

These small, brightly colored berries are closely related to the black currant. An offshoot of the red currant is the white currant — both of which grow on shrubs. Unripe currants can be used in cooking and, although they do not require as much sweetening as may be expected, they go well with honey. Red currants can be combined with black currants, raspberries, strawberries, loganberries and cherries in a delicious jam. Red currants can be crystallized or frosted by dipping in egg white and then dusting with superfine sugar and leaving to dry. In little bunches, these make an attractive decoration.

Pomegranates

The larger the fruit the better the flavor. They should be crimson, brownish red or bright red. Cut through the skin all the way around, then break them open. The seeds can be sucked of flesh and then discarded, or they can be eaten. The flesh around the seeds, however, is regarded as the edible part. The white pith is bitter and should not be eaten.

Tamarillos

When ripe, tamarillos should be firm but not hard. They can be cut in half and eaten with a spoon, but if you are cooking them, the skin must be removed as it is bitter. Pour boiling water over them, leave for 2 minutes, after which the skin will peel off, just like a tomato. They make a delicious sauce for smoked meats, pork and lamb.

Papayas

When buying papayas, avoid any with shriveled skin or bruises. The fragrance is a good indicator or ripeness. Cut into wedges, remove the seeds, squeeze lime juice over them, and eat chilled for breakfast. Papayas can also be added to fruit salads, or made into a sorbet. Papaya is a natural meat tenderizer so you can mix it with meat for an hour or so before you cook it, to make it more succulent.

Kiwifruit

This fruit with its hairy, egg-shaped appearance originally came from China, and was known as a Chinese gooseberry. Most kiwifruit comes from New Zealand, hence its name. The kiwifruit has a green flesh and a mass of tiny black seeds. The flesh is ideal for use in ice creams and sorbets and surprisingly is also a good meat tenderizer. The color of the kiwifruit also makes it a very attractive decoration for fruit dishes and desserts.

Coconut

Coconut cream with its creamy, thick base is an exquisite addition to curries, adding texture and flavor. Coconut cream is easily made by puréeing 2 cups of water with 1 cup of grated coconut meat and then straining the purée. To collect the water in the coconut without having it splattered everywhere, pierce two of the eyes and pour out the water. Then split the shell open with a hammer. The white meat can be grated in a blender. One coconut produces about 4 cups of grated coconut.

Loquat

Ginger, lemon juice and crystallized fruit go well with loquats. They can be eaten fresh and also used in fruit compotes, made into jams, and preserved. Loquats with their yellow to yellow-orange skin, are available in spring and early summer.

Kumquat

Similar in appearance to a very small orange, kumquats are seen in the stores in winter. Kumquats are eaten raw, skin and all, and make an interesting addition to rice dishes and green salads. Jams and chutneys are another usual preparation for this fruit. A true delicacy is kumquats left to soak in sugar syrup and brandy for a few months. The brandied fruit can then be used in desserts and the brandy as a delightful drink.

Dates

Dried dates are almost considered a staple, but now fresh dates are becoming more and more available in greengrocers and ethnic markets. The very sweet flavor of dates lends this fruit to being used in cakes and desserts. Dates make an interesting addition to rice dishes and curries and are a delicious accompaniment to spiced and cold meats. More exotic preparations include pitted dates stuffed with fondant, nuts, especially almonds, crystallized fruits or marzipan.

Figs

Figs vary in colors from white or green to red-purple and black. Fresh figs need not be peeled before being eaten, unless the skin is very thick. Dried figs are considerably sweeter with the sugar content increasing by over 30 per cent. In Italy and Greece fresh figs are served as an antipasto with slices of meat such as prosciutto or on their own with freshly ground black pepper. Ginger, cream, nuts, cinnamon and citrus fruits all go well with figs. Liqueurs are another interesting addition to this sugary, syrupy, uniquely flavored fruit.

Soups

Soups are no longer relegated to the appetizer menu; they are becoming increasingly popular as a main course. A big bowl of minestrone, sprinkled with Parmesan, eaten with crusty bread and followed by a salad, is a balanced, nutritious and sustaining meal. Lighter soups, such as cream of vegetable soups, can also be the main part of a meal, but since they are much less sustaining and nutritious, they should be accompanied by a sandwich or a mixed salad.

Most soups require stock as their basis. Stock cubes can be used but be aware of how much salt is in them. If you don't make your own, chicken or beef stock can be bought canned or frozen. Or use vegetable stock, made by keeping the water in which you've cooked your vegetables.

Making soup is much easier than it once was if you have a blender or food processor. Be careful though that you don't put too much liquid in at one time or it will drip down the sides and all over the kitchen table. It's better to remove the vegetables from the saucepan with a slotted spoon and add just a little of the stock to the food processor before you purée.

BEAN AND PEA SOUP

¼ cup kidney beans

¼ cup lima beans

¼ cup yellow split peas

¼ cup chick peas

3 tablespoons oil

1 onion, chopped

½ cup chopped red pepper

¼ cup chopped celery

¼ cup chopped carrots

1½ tablespoons chopped parsley

1 clove garlic, crushed

4½ cups stock (beef, chicken or vegetable)

1 bay leaf

pinch of marjoram

pinch of basil

½ cup chopped peeled tomatoes

Soak beans and peas overnight in water to cover. Next day, cook in the water until they are tender and discard the liquid. The chick peas will take longer to cook than the other legumes.

Heat the oil in a large saucepan and add the onion, pepper, celery, carrot, parsley and garlic. Cook, stirring for 5 minutes or until the onion is soft. Add the stock and simmer until the vegetables are tender.

Add the beans and peas and all the remaining ingredients and simmer for 20 minutes. Remove the bay leaf before serving.

SERVES 4

CREAMED OYSTER SOUP

4 dozen oysters, freshly shucked (or canned and drained)

2 cups milk

2 cups cream

½ teaspoon celery seeds

1 tablespoon finely chopped celery leaves

freshly ground black pepper

dash Worcestershire sauce

pinch of cayenne

Mix the oysters with the milk and cream. Add celery seeds and leaves, pepper and Worcestershire sauce. Bring almost to the boil, simmer until the oysters are heated through and plump, dust with cayenne and serve.

SERVES 4–6

CHINESE GREEN SOUP

1 tablespoon oil

½ teaspoon grated ginger root

1 clove garlic, crushed

5 cups hot chicken or vegetable stock

1 cup rice

1 head Chinese cabbage, finely shredded (about 1½ pounds)

6 scallions, finely chopped

1 tablespoon dry sherry

¾ teaspoon sesame oil

Heat the oil in a saucepan and sauté the ginger and garlic for 1 minute. Pour in the hot stock and add the rice. Simmer for 15 minutes or until the rice is just tender. Add the cabbage and scallions and simmer for 5 minutes. Stir in the sherry and sesame oil and serve.

SERVES 4–6

SPICY CHICKEN AND AVOCADO SOUP

6 cups chicken stock

1 whole chicken breast

2 onions, thinly sliced

½ teaspoon dried coriander

½ teaspoon dried oregano

1 teaspoon curry powder

freshly ground black pepper

1 large avocado

Put the chicken stock into a saucepan with the chicken breast, onions and seasonings. Bring to the boil and simmer for 15 minutes. Remove chicken, strain the stock and discard the onion. Remove the skin from the chicken and slice the meat into thin strips. Return it to the stock, heat, but do not allow it to boil.

Peel the avocado and slice thinly. Place slices in individual soup bowls and pour the soup over. The slices will float on top. Serve immediately before the avocado begins to brown.

SERVES 6

GAZPACHO ON ICE

6 cloves garlic

1 tablespoon sugar

3 tablespoons paprika

½ cup olive oil

3 tablespoons wine vinegar

pinch of cayenne

One 28-ounce can tomatoes

4 cups chicken stock

1 cucumber, peeled and diced

24 scallions, finely sliced

1–2 green peppers, cut into tiny cubes

Put the garlic, sugar, paprika, oil, vinegar and cayenne into a blender and purée. Add the tomatoes and blend again.

Combine the blended ingredients and the stock in a large bowl. Add the diced cucumber to the soup and cover with plastic. Chill until ready to serve.

To serve, pour the soup over ice cubes in individual bowls and sprinkle with chopped scallions and pepper.

SERVES 8

COLD YOGURT AND CUCUMBER SOUP

1 cucumber, peeled and diced

2 cups chicken stock

2 cloves garlic, crushed

2 cups yogurt

juice ½ lemon

pinch of dried coriander

1 cup iced water

4–6 very thin lemon slices (optional)

2 tablespoons chopped walnuts (optional)

Gazpacho On Ice (above) and Cold Yogurt and Cucumber Soup

Put cucumber and stock in a saucepan and simmer until the cucumber is just tender. Chill.

Combine the garlic, yogurt, lemon juice and coriander. Stir into the chilled soup with iced water. Serve topped with lemon slices and sprinkled with chopped walnuts.

SERVES 4–6

LEMON SOUP

1 egg yolk

3 tablespoons lemon juice

2 cups canned chicken broth

1 cup water

5 tablespoons cooked rice

3 tablespoons finely chopped fresh parsley

Beat the egg yolk with lemon juice. Heat the soup with water and add rice. Slowly add a little hot soup to the egg-lemon mixture and then pour it back into the soup. Season to taste and decorate with chopped parsley.

SERVES 4

ICED BUTTERMILK SOUP

1 small cucumber

salt

3 cups stock (chicken or vegetable)

3 cups buttermilk

1 teaspoon Dijon mustard

2 tablespoons minced celery

2 teaspoons chopped chives

2 teaspoons chopped fresh dill

2 teaspoons chopped fresh parsley

Peel and finely dice the cucumber. Place it in a colander, sprinkle with salt and allow to stand for

30 minutes. Rinse the cucumber in cold water to remove excess salt and dry on paper towels.

Place the cucumber in a large bowl, add the remaining ingredients and mix well. Chill before serving.

SERVES 4–6

COUNTRY HARVEST SOUP

¼ cup whole wheat grain

3 tablespoons butter

1 small onion, finely chopped

1 cup walnuts

1½ cups chicken or vegetable stock

1 bouquet garni

1 tablespoon flour

¼ teaspoon dry mustard

2 cups milk

1½ cups Cheddar cheese, grated

2 tablespoons cream (optional)

Soak the wheat in boiling water for 1 hour. Melt half the butter in a large saucepan and sauté the onion until it is soft but not brown. Grind the walnuts on a board with a rolling pin. Drain the wheat and add it to the pan with the walnuts, stock and bouquet garni. Bring to the boil, cover and simmer for about 1 hour, or until the wheat is tender. Remove bouquet garni.

Melt the remaining butter in a separate pan, stir in the flour and mustard and cook for 2 minutes, stirring continuously. Remove the pan from the heat and gradually add the milk, stirring continuously. Slowly bring to the boil and simmer for 3 minutes, still stirring.

Add the sauce to the wheat mixture with the grated cheese and season to taste. Heat gently, without boiling and stir in the cream if used.

SERVES 6

CHILLED PUMPKIN SOUP

2 pounds pumpkin, peeled and
   diced

4½ cups chicken stock

1 onion, chopped

4 scallions, sliced

¼ cup cream

freshly ground black pepper

chives, to garnish

Cook pumpkin in water until tender.
Drain, cool and purée in a blender
or food processor. Simmer the
stock with onion and scallions for
15 minutes, cool and strain.

Mix the pumpkin into the stock,
season to taste, serve with a swirl
of cream, cover and chill. Garnish
with chives.

SERVES 6

PEA AND BARLEY SOUP

½ cup barley

2 cups water

4 cups stock (chicken, vegetable
   or beef)

1½ tablespoons butter

1 tablespoon flour

freshly ground black pepper

½ cup milk

1 carrot, peeled and cut in strips

1 cup green peas

1 tablespoon chopped chives, to
   garnish

Soak the barley in the water
overnight. Drain, rinse and place in
a saucepan with the stock. Cover
and simmer for 1 hour or until the
barley is tender. Strain, reserving
4 tablespoons of the cooked barley.
Use the rest of the barley for
another dish.

Chilled Pumpkin Soup

Melt the butter and stir in the flour
and pepper. Cook for 1 minute, then
add the strained stock and bring to
the boil, stirring constantly.

Add the milk and reserved barley
and simmer while you prepare the
vegetables.

Cook the carrot with the peas in
water until just tender. Drain and
add to the soup. Serve garnished
with chives.

SERVES 4

LENTIL SOUP

½ pound lentils

1 onion, finely chopped

1 clove garlic, crushed

2 tablespoons parsley, finely
   chopped

2 tablespoons oil

2 large tomatoes, peeled, seeded
   and chopped

2 tablespoons white wine vinegar
   (optional)

Soak the lentils in water for 1 hour.
Simmer in the same water for
1 hour. Sauté the onion, garlic
and parsley in the oil until the onion
is soft but not brown. Add the
tomatoes and cook for 5 minutes.

Combine the tomato mixture with
the lentils and reheat before serving.
Add vinegar if using. It gives a
pleasantly sharp taste to the soup.

SERVES 4-6

WATERCRESS AND VERMICELLI SOUP

1 small bunch watercress

2 onions, sliced

4½ cups chicken stock

¾ cup vermicelli

Wash the watercress thoroughly
and discard the stalks. Place the
watercress, onion and stock in a pan
and simmer for 15 minutes. Add
the vermicelli and simmer for
2 minutes or until tender. Pour
into a serving dish.

SERVES 4-6

ICED CLODNICK

One 15-ounce can sliced beets

1 cup sour cream

2 cups cold white wine

1 cucumber, peeled and diced

¼ pound cooked peeled shrimp

freshly ground black pepper

2 tablespoons finely chopped fresh
   dill

In a large bowl, whisk together the
juice from the beets, the sour cream
and wine. Dice the beets and add to
the liquid with the cucumber. Add
the shrimp and season to taste.

Cover with plastic wrap and chill
until needed. To serve, pour over
ice cubes in individual bowls and
sprinkle with dill.

SERVES 4-6

CARROT AND ORANGE SOUP

1¾ pounds carrots, sliced

1 onion, chopped

2 sticks celery, chopped

4 cups chicken or vegetable stock

1 bay leaf

1 tablespoon cornstarch

grated rind and juice of 1 orange

pinch of nutmeg

freshly ground black pepper

¼ cup cream

bay leaves, to garnish

Place the carrots, celery and onion in a pan with the stock and bay leaf. Cover and simmer for 20 minutes until tender. Purée the vegetables in a blender or through a sieve. Blend the cornstarch with a little of the stock and return it to the saucepan with the puréed vegetables, orange rind and juice and nutmeg. Season to taste.

Bring to the boil and simmer for 3 minutes, stirring. Pour soup into a serving bowl and decorate with a swirl of cream. Garnish with bay leaves.

SERVES 4–6

CREAM OF CHAYOTE SOUP

6 chayotes

1 onion, chopped

1 stalk celery, stringed and chopped

½ cup rice

7 cups stock (chicken or vegetable)

1 clove garlic, crushed

Clockwise from top: Cream of Chayote Soup, Fresh Tomato Soup and Carrot and Orange Soup

freshly ground black pepper

½ cup sour cream (optional)

sweet pepper, cut in strips

Peel the chayotes, remove the seed and chop roughly. Place chayotes, onion, celery, rice, stock, garlic and ground pepper in a large saucepan. Simmer for 45 minutes.

Cool and purée the soup in a blender, or through a sieve. Return mixture to saucepan. Stir in the sour cream over low heat. Do not allow it to boil. Serve hot with a dollop of sour cream if desired. Garnish with strips of pepper.

SERVES 4–6

FRESH TOMATO SOUP

2 tablespoons butter or margarine

1 onion, thinly sliced

1 carrot, peeled and thinly sliced

1 tablespoon plain flour

2 pounds tomatoes, peeled and quartered

3 cups chicken or vegetable stock

1 bay leaf

pinch of ground mace

freshly ground black pepper

fresh rosemary, to garnish

Melt butter in a heavy, medium pot. Add onion and carrot. Cover and cook over low heat for 5 to 10 minutes. Remove pan from heat. Stir in flour. Add tomatoes, stock, bay leaf, mace and seasoning. Bring to boil, stirring. Simmer, covered, for 20 to 30 minutes.

Purée the soup either in a food processor or blender, or by pressing through a sieve. Rinse out pot and return puréed soup. Reheat before serving. Garnish with rosemary.

SERVES 6

CHILLED GREEN PEA SOUP

2 cups frozen peas

4 lettuce leaves, shredded

1 cup chopped scallions

1 cup water

2 cups chicken stock

4 tablespoons sour cream or yogurt

1 tablespoon chopped fresh mint

Bring peas, lettuce and scallions to the boil in the water. Lower the heat, cover and simmer for 8 minutes. Purée in a blender or food processor.

Transfer to a bowl and blend in the chicken stock. Cover and chill until needed. To serve, stir in the sour cream or yogurt and decorate with mint.

SERVES 4–6

ICED ORANGE AND TOMATO SOUP

3¾ cups canned tomato juice, well chilled

1 cup freshly squeezed orange juice

1 tablespoon grated orange rind

1 cup cream

freshly ground black pepper

1 avocado

lemon juice

Place the tomato juice, orange juice, orange rind and cream in a blender and mix well. Season to taste.

Peel the avocado, remove the pit and slice the flesh thinly. Pour over a little lemon juice to prevent it from browning.

Serve the soup in individual bowls over ice cubes with avocado slices.

SERVES 4–6

ICED BEET SOUP

4½ cups water

2 cloves garlic

½ bunch celery, finely chopped

1 small onion, chopped

2 tomatoes, peeled and chopped

One 16-ounce can sliced beets

2 tablespoons red wine vinegar

2 tablespoons sugar

3 tablespoons lemon juice

3 egg yolks, beaten

1¼ cups sour cream

snipped chives, to garnish

Place the water in a saucepan with garlic, celery, onion, tomatoes, beets, vinegar and sugar. Bring to the boil then lower the heat and simmer for 15 minutes. Remove from the heat, cool slightly, then pour into a blender or food processor and purée. (You may have to do this in 2 batches.) Strain soup.

Clockwise from top: Chilled Green Pea Soup, Iced Orange and Tomato Soup and Iced Beet Soup

Return the soup to the saucepan, place over very low heat, stir in the lemon juice and egg yolks until the soup is slightly thickened. Do not allow it to boil.

Cool, then cover and chill until needed. To serve, stir in sour cream until well blended and sprinkle with chives.

SERVES 6

MINESTRONE

⅓ cup cannellini or any small white beans

⅓ cup whole dried peas

9 cups chicken or vegetable stock

1 large stalk celery, chopped

1 large onion, sliced

2 medium carrots, sliced

2 tomatoes, peeled and quartered

½ cup any leafy green vegetable, sliced

½ teaspoon dried basil

Minestrone

½ teaspoon dried oregano

½ cup macaroni

⅓ cup grated Parmesan cheese

chopped parsley to garnish

Soak the beans and peas together overnight in 3 cups of stock. The beans should be white and plump, the peas green and plump. Discard any that are hard, brown or wrinkled.

Add the peas, beans and their soaking stock to the remaining stock with the celery, onion and carrots in a large pan. Bring to the boil and simmer for 1–2 hours or until the beans and peas are tender. Add the tomatoes, leafy vegetable, basil and oregano. Cook for 10 minutes.

Add macaroni and cook for 10–15 minutes until it is tender. Serve with grated cheese and garnish with parsley.

SERVES 6

First Courses

Most of the recipes in this chapter can double up as main courses for a light meal. Or you can serve them with other first courses or salads to make a one course meal consisting of several different things.

This way of eating is starting to make sense to many cooks. It's more casual than the traditional two or three course meals, and less work and strain for the cook. If everything is placed on the table at the same time the cook can sit down and eat with everyone else and not have to worry again until it's time for fruit or dessert.

Some of the dishes in this chapter, however, such as Brains in Black Butter, should be eaten by themselves, with no accompaniment whatever.

SPANAKOPITA

2 pounds fresh spinach

7 eggs

½ pound feta cheese, crumbled

1½ cups grated Cheddar cheese

oil

1 onion, chopped

freshly ground black pepper

pinch of dried oregano

8 sheets filo pastry

7 tablespoons butter

Wash the spinach well, chop it coarsely and put it into a large pan. Cover the pan and cook the spinach over low heat for 7–8 minutes or until it is wilted. Drain well in a colander, pressing out the moisture with a wooden spoon. Beat the eggs until fluffy and add the feta and Cheddar.

Heat a little oil in a pan and sauté the onion until it is golden. Add the spinach, egg-cheese mixture, pepper and a little oregano.

Preheat the oven to 375°F. Melt the butter and brush a baking dish with it. Lay a sheet of filo pastry on top and brush it with butter. Top with another 4 sheets, brushing each with melted butter and turning each sheet slightly so that the corners fan out, rather than stacking them on top of each other. Reserve 3 sheets.

Pour in the spinach mixture and fold the pastry ends over it. Butter the reserved sheets of filo and place them on the top to cover the dish. Slash the pastry in a few places with a sharp knife to allow the steam to escape. Brush the top with more melted butter and bake for 45 minutes.

SERVES 8

MELON AMBROSIA

1 cantaloupe

1 honeydew melon

DRESSING

2 teaspoons Dijon mustard

1 teaspoon lemon juice

¼ teaspoon vanilla extract

6 tablespoons honey

⅔ cup mayonnaise

⅓ cup heavy cream

Cut melons in half and scoop out seeds. Use a melon baller to make as many melon balls as you can. Mix them together in a large bowl.

To make the dressing, blend mustard with lemon juice and vanilla, stir in honey, mayonnaise and cream. Serve drizzled over the melon balls.

SERVES 6–8

BRAINS IN BLACK BUTTER

4 sets brains

4 tablespoons vinegar

1 large onion, spiked with 4 cloves

1 bay leaf

2 tablespoons flour

7 tablespoons butter

1 tablespoon capers

Soak the brains in salted water for 1 hour, then remove and discard the membranes. Place the brains in a saucepan and cover with fresh water. Add vinegar, onion and bay leaf, bring to the boil and simmer for 15 minutes. Set aside in the water, until ready to cook.

Remove the brains from the liquid, pat them dry with a cloth, dust lightly with flour and gently pan-fry in lots of foaming butter, turning only once.

When cooked, remove them with a slotted spoon and place on warmed plates. Allow the butter to cook briskly until it is dark, but not black. Add the capers with a little of their brine to the pan and pour over the brains. Serve immediately with toast triangles.

SERVES 4

HERBED JELLIED MEAT LOAF

1 cup mixed fresh herbs (parsley, tarragon and chives)

1½ pounds cooked meat (chicken, turkey, ham, tongue or beef)

2 tablespoons green peppercorns, rinsed in cold water

2 cups chicken stock

2 tablespoons gelatin

½ cup white wine

juice 1 lemon

shredded lettuce, to serve

Finely chop the herbs and the meat and mix them with the green peppercorns. Put the stock into a saucepan and simmer. Dissolve the gelatin in the wine and add to the stock with the lemon juice. Pour it over the meat mixture.

Lightly oil a loaf pan and spoon the mixture into it. Tap the pan on the table to eliminate air bubbles. Allow to cool, then chill until set.

To unmold, run a warm knife around the edges of the pan, cover with a serving dish and turn upside down. Surround with shredded lettuce and serve in slices.

SERVES 6–8

VEGETABLE PÂTÉ

1 leek, well washed

2 cups shelled peas

4 cups shredded spinach

1 egg

½ teaspoon dried tarragon

¼ teaspoon nutmeg

3 cups sliced carrots

freshly ground black pepper

4 tablespoons butter

½ cup water

2 tablespoons flour

Slice the white part of the leek into thin rounds and steam until tender. Line a loaf pan with oiled wax paper and place the cooked leek on top, smoothing it down to make a thin layer.

Cook the peas in boiling water and steam the spinach over them. When the peas are tender, drain them and combine with the spinach, egg, tarragon and nutmeg in a blender or food processor and purée. Spoon the spinach/pea mixture over the leeks and smooth out the top with a spatula.

Cook the carrots with pepper, butter and water until they are tender. Drain off any remaining liquid and purée the carrots with the flour. Spoon the carrot purée over the spinach in the loaf tin and smooth the top with a spatula. Rap the pan on the table to remove any air bubbles.

Preheat oven to 350°F. Place wax paper over the pâté and cover with 3–4 layers of foil. Bake for 1½ hours. Allow the pâté to chill for 2 hours before turning out onto a serving dish. This pâté is delicious served with a sauce made from onions, garlic and tomatoes.

SERVES 4

HOT CHEESE BALLS

4 tablespoons butter

½ teaspoon prepared English mustard

freshly ground black pepper

5 tablespoons flour

2 cups milk

6 ounces Gruyère cheese

cornstarch

2 eggs, beaten

dry breadcrumbs, to coat

oil for deep-frying

Melt the butter in a saucepan with the mustard and pepper. Stir in the flour and gradually add the milk. Continue stirring until the sauce thickens and boils. Pour the sauce into a bowl, cover with plastic wrap and cool.

Sprinkle a baking sheet with cornstarch. Cut the cheese into 12 equal-sized cubes. Dip the cheese

into the sauce so that each piece is coated and place them on the tray. Chill the balls until they are set.

Roll the cheese balls in beaten egg, then coat with breadcrumbs. Chill for half an hour.

Heat the oil and deep-fry the balls until golden brown. Drain and serve immediately.

MAKES 12 BALLS

Left: Vegetable Pâté and Hot Cheese Balls
Top: Shrimp Pâté (left) and Eggplant Purée

EGGPLANT PURÉE

2 eggplants

juice 1 lemon

1 tablespoon oil

2 cloves garlic, crushed

4 ounces cream cheese

2 tablespoons yogurt

black olives for decoration

paprika, to garnish

Preheat oven to 350°F. Place eggplants on a baking sheet and cook for 1 hour. Cut in half, scoop out the pulp and purée it in a blender or food processor.

Add the lemon juice, oil, garlic, cream cheese and yogurt. Blend until smooth. Place in a bowl and chill for several hours. Garnish with olives and paprika. Eggplant purée can be served in the scooped out eggplant cases.

SERVES 6–8

SHRIMP PÂTÉ

1 pound shrimp, cooked and peeled

3 tablespoons lemon juice

½ cup olive oil

freshly ground black pepper

pinch of paprika

dill, to garnish

Place the shrimp in a blender or food processor with the lemon juice and purée. Slowly add the oil until well blended. Add the seasonings. Chill until needed. Garnish with dill and serve with dry toast fingers.

SERVES 6

TOMATO GRANITA

8 tomatoes, peeled, and finely chopped

2 scallions, finely chopped

1 stalk celery, finely chopped

1 clove garlic, crushed

1 cucumber

1 teaspoon chopped fresh mint

mint leaves for decoration

Strain the tomatoes to remove excess liquid and seeds. Mix the scallions, celery and garlic with the tomatoes and pour into ice cream trays. Freeze until solid.

Ten minutes before serving, remove from the freezer to soften a little. Peel the cucumber and chop into very fine dice. Break up the tomato ice with a fork and stir in the cucumber and mint. Serve in individual glass dishes. Garnish with mint leaves.

SERVES 4

Tomato Granita

ASPARAGUS WITH HERBS AND PARMESAN

Try to buy thick asparagus for this dish. However, if thin asparagus is all that's available, each diner will need 6 spears instead of 4, the stalks will not need peeling and the cooking time should be reduced to 7–9 minutes.

16 thick asparagus spears

5 tablespoons butter

1 clove garlic, finely chopped

1½ tablespoons finely chopped fresh parsley

1½ tablespoons finely chopped chives

1½ tablespoons lemon juice

grated Parmesan cheese

Using a vegetable peeler, peel the lower part of the stalks, cut off the ends and wash the asparagus well in cold running water. Tie them into 2 bundles with string and place them in an asparagus steamer or a large pan of boiling water. The stalks only should be in the water so that the tips steam. Cover the pan with foil or an upturned saucepan of the same diameter. Cook for 8–12 minutes, depending upon the thickness of the asparagus. Test after 7 minutes; the thickest part of the stalk should be just tender. Overcooking ruins asparagus.

Drain and keep warm in a folded napkin. Melt the butter in a small pan over medium heat. Add the garlic, cook gently and stir in the herbs and lemon juice.

Place asparagus on warmed plates and spoon over the sauce. Serve Parmesan separately.

SERVES 4

Asparagus With Herbs and Parmesan

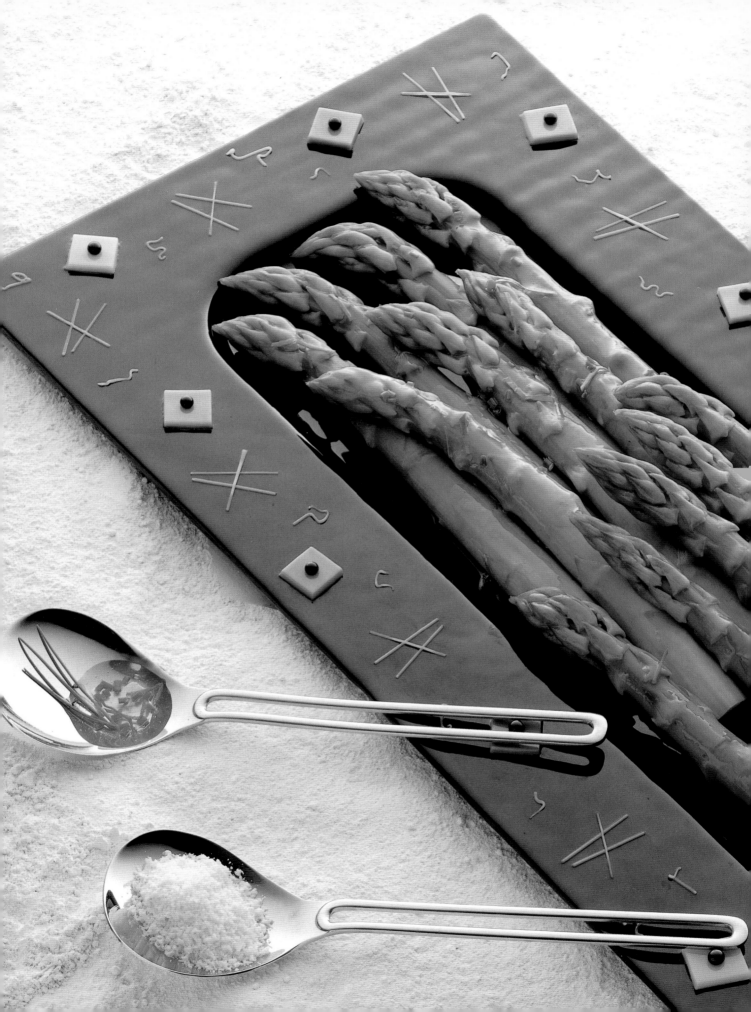

SPANISH-STYLE SARDINES

1 pound sardines, smelts or other small whole fish

olive oil, for shallow-frying

4 tablespoons flour

1 egg, beaten

lemon rind for decoration

oregano, to garnish

MARINADE

1 teaspoon dry mustard

½ teaspoon freshly ground black pepper

1½ tablespoons chopped fresh parsley

½ teaspoon dried oregano

4 tablespoons olive oil

juice ½ lemon

1½ tablespoons chopped anchovy fillets

Split the sardines on one side and pull out the backbone with the tail section. Remove heads, rinse and dry.

Mix marinade ingredients together and pour over fish. Let sit least 1 hour.

Heat the oil, remove the sardines from the marinade, dust very lightly with flour and dip into beaten egg. Fry quickly and serve hot, garnished with lemon rind and oregano.

SERVES 4

GRILLED MUSHROOM CAPS

1 pound medium-sized mushrooms

2–4 cloves garlic, crushed

5 tablespoons butter

2½ tablespoons grated Parmesan cheese

5 tablespoons breadcrumbs

4 slices bacon, trimmed and diced

Wipe mushrooms and carefully remove the stems. Chop the stems finely and mix them with the crushed garlic.

Grilled Mushroom Caps and Spanish-style Sardines

1 tablespoon tomato purée

¼ teaspoon cayenne

chile, shredded, to garnish

Combine rice, cheese, chives and carrot in a bowl. Mix in the flour, chili powder and pepper. Separate the eggs and beat the yolks into the rice mixture. Beat the whites until stiff and fold into the rice mixture. Heat the oil for deep-frying and drop teaspoons of the mixture into it. Deep-fry until golden brown and serve warm with tomato sauce.

To make the tomato sauce, whisk all ingredients together until smooth. Chill before serving. Garnish with shredded chile.

SERVES 4

HERBED GREEN BEANS

1 stick butter

½ teaspoon chopped fresh
  marjoram

½ teaspoon fresh basil

1 teaspoon chopped fresh parsley

1 teaspoon chopped chives

1 pound green beans

1 small onion, chopped

1 clove garlic, chopped

freshly ground black pepper

¼ cup sunflower seeds, to serve

fresh chives, to garnish

Combine butter with marjoram, basil, parsley and chives and set aside. Place the beans in a saucepan with the onion and garlic and cover with boiling water. Cook until tender and drain. Add herb butter to the pan and swirl the beans around briefly until well coated. Season to taste and add sunflower seeds just before serving. Tie beans into bundles with chives before serving.

SERVES 6

Herbed Green Beans (above) and Rice Croquettes with Tomato Sauce

Mash the butter with a fork and mix in the cheese, breadcrumbs and mushroom stalks. Fry or broil the bacon until crisp, drain on kitchen paper and add to the cheese mixture.

Fill the mushrooms caps with the mixture and place under a hot broiler to brown quickly.

SERVES 4–6

RICE CROQUETTES WITH TOMATO SAUCE

2 cups cooked brown rice

½ cup grated Swiss cheese

1 tablespoon chopped chives

1 tablespoon grated carrot

1 tablespoon self-rising flour

¼ teaspoon chili powder

freshly ground black pepper

2 eggs

oil for deep-frying

TOMATO SAUCE

¼ cup mayonnaise

¼ cup yogurt

¼ cup sour cream

PIQUANT APRICOTS

½ pound fresh apricots

4 ounces cream cheese

2½ tablespoons mayonnaise

5 tablespoons chopped chives

1 tablespoon chopped fresh
    parsley

cayenne

¼ red pepper

fresh lettuce leaves

Cut the apricots in half and remove
their pits. Beat the cheese with the
mayonnaise and stir in the chives,
parsley and pepper.

Spoon the mixture into the apricot
halves. Cut the pepper into thin
strips and use it to garnish the
apricots. Serve on a bed of shredded
lettuce or in lettuce cups.

SERVES 4

POTATOES CZARINA

6 large potatoes, baked in their
    skins

3 tablespoons butter

freshly ground black pepper

⅔ cup sour cream

small jar caviar or lumpfish roe

1 onion, finely chopped

Cut the tops off the baked potatoes
and carefully scoop out the pulp into
a warmed bowl. Keep the oven
warm at 350°F. Mash, season and
add butter and sour cream.

Carefully fold in caviar and onion
and return to the potato cases. Heat
through in the oven.

SERVES 6

BROAD BEAN PÂTÉ

2 pounds broad beans, shelled
    (about 2 cups)

4 ounces cream cheese

3 tablespoons chopped fresh
    parsley

juice 1 lemon

freshly ground black pepper

Cook the shelled beans in boiling
water until soft. Drain and pound to
a paste with a wooden spoon or in a
food processor. Beat in the cheese,
parsley, lemon juice and pepper.
Press into an earthenware bowl.
Chill and serve with hot toast.

SERVES 6-8

SHRIMP RASCALS

1 cup chopped cooked shrimp

1 tart apple, peeled and diced

½ cup chopped celery

¼ cup sliced radishes

1 tablespoon dried onion flakes

½ cup mayonnaise

4 tablespoons cream

1 tablespoon horseradish cream

2 tablespoons chopped walnuts

2–3 tomatoes, thickly sliced

freshly ground black pepper

1 tablespoon finely chopped fresh
    dill

Combine the shrimp with the apple
and fresh vegetables in a bowl. In
a separate bowl mix together the
onion flakes, mayonnaise, cream,
horseradish and walnuts. Add this
to the shrimp mixture and season
to taste.

To serve, place a spoonful of the
shrimp mixture on top of each
tomato slice and sprinkle with dill.

SERVES 4-6

POTATO SOUFFLÉ

1 pound boiled potatoes

1½ tablespoons butter

4 tablespoons cream

3 egg yolks, beaten

freshly ground black pepper

4 tablespoons grated Cheddar
    cheese

4 egg whites, stiffly beaten

Mash potatoes well with butter and
cream. Add the beaten egg yolks,
season to taste and stir in most of
the cheese, retaining a little for the
topping.

Preheat the oven to 375°F. Fold in
stiffly beaten egg whites. Pour into
a buttered soufflé dish and sprinkle
with the remaining cheese. Bake for
25 minutes and serve immediately
from the soufflé dish.

SERVES 4-6

TOMATOES ROQUEFORT

4 tomatoes, thinly sliced

1 onion, thinly sliced into rings

1 tablespoon chopped fresh
    parsley

½ cup Roquefort cheese

2 tablespoons olive oil

2 tablespoons lemon juice

1 teaspoon sugar

freshly ground black pepper

pinch of paprika

Place the tomatoes on a serving dish
and cover with a layer of onion
rings. Blend all the remaining
ingredients until creamy and pour
over the tomato/onion base. Chill
before serving.

SERVES 4

STUFFED TURNIPS

4 small turnips

3 tablespoons butter

sprig fresh rosemary

1 cup mashed potato

2 tablespoons grated onion

freshly ground black pepper

2 teaspoons chopped fresh parsley

juice 1 lemon

Wash the turnips, peel them, but do not cut off the base. Cook the turnips in boiling water until tender but still firm. Cut a lid off each one and scoop out the center, leaving the outer part as a cup. Reserve the pulp.

Melt the butter in a frying pan and crumble the rosemary into it. Place the turnip cups in the pan and cook for 1 minute.

Preheat the oven to 400°F. Mash the turnip pulp with the potato and add the grated onion and pepper. Spoon the filling back into the turnip cases, place in a baking dish and sprinkle with parsley and lemon juice. Bake for 10 minutes.

SERVES 4

STUFFED ARTICHOKES

4 artichokes

4 lemon slices

2 tablespoons white wine vinegar

6 hard-boiled eggs, chopped

3 scallions, chopped

5 tomatoes, peeled, seeded and chopped

DRESSING

⅔ cup yogurt

1 teaspoon honey

1 teaspoon Dijon mustard

1 tablespoon oil

juice of 1 lemon

1 tablespoon chopped fresh parsley

Remove the stems from the artichokes and cut the base flush so that it will sit up straight on a plate. Using a very sharp knife, cut the top off the artichoke, about ¼ of the way down.

Stand each artichoke on a slice of lemon in a saucepan and cook in boiling salted water for 15–20 minutes, or until a leaf pulls out easily. Drain.

To make the dressing, blend the yogurt, honey, mustard, oil, lemon and parsley. Combine with the eggs, scallions and tomatoes.

Gently open the artichoke leaves to reveal the hairy choke in the center. Scoop this out with a teaspoon and discard. Spoon the filling into the artichoke hearts and serve at room temperature or slightly chilled.

To eat, break off the leaves, one by one, starting with the large outside leaves. Dip the base of the leaf into the filling and pull the leaf between your teeth, eating only the fleshy base and discarding the stringy leaf tops.

SERVES 4

Stuffed Artichokes

Salads

*M*ost of the salads in this chapter are main courses in themselves. Made in smaller quantities, they can also be served as a first course.

The flavor of many salads is improved if they are served warm or at room temperature instead of cold. Chicken salad, for example, is delicious if served at room temperature; it suffers badly once it has been chilled. The same applies to seafood salads. However, if a salad is not to be chilled, it must be served soon after it is made, especially in summer.

There are no recipes here for simple green salads, although these are mentioned often in the menus at the back of the book. To make a green salad, wash lettuce leaves, either one type or several types such as romaine, leaf and butter, drain them well in a colander, salad basket or, best of all, salad twirler, tear the leaves and dress with a mixture of oil and vinegar or lemon juice. The usual proportions are 5 parts oil to 1 part vinegar, but you can change that to suit your own taste. Add mustard if you like, with salt and pepper. A more complicated green salad includes chicory, endive, spinach, watercress or any other green leaves. The torn leaves of fresh herbs, especially parsley, basil and salad burnet, make a delicious addition.

POPPY SEED SALAD

1 lettuce

4 spinach leaves

1 cucumber, peeled and diced

½ green pepper, thinly sliced

½ cup chopped scallions

DRESSING

¼ cup sugar

2 teaspoons dry mustard

3 tablespoons lemon juice

4 tablespoons poppy seeds

1 cup white wine vinegar

¾ cup olive oil

Wash lettuce and spinach thoroughly and tear into bite-sized pieces. Combine with cucumber, pepper and scallions in a salad bowl and refrigerate while preparing the dressing.

Mix together sugar, mustard, lemon juice, poppy seeds and vinegar. Gradually beat in the oil until the dressing is thick.

Use as much dressing as required for the salad and store the rest in a screw top jar.

SERVES 4

TROPICAL RICE SALAD

1 head lettuce

2 cups cooked brown rice

1 cup chopped pineapple

¼ cup chopped celery

¼ cup chopped scallions

¼ cup chopped red pepper

¼ cup whole cooked corn kernels

¼ cup chopped walnuts

1 red apple

2 tablespoons lemon juice

1 tomato

1 tablespoon chopped fresh parsley

Wash the lettuce and line a salad bowl with the best leaves. Shred the remaining lettuce. Mix together the rice, pineapple, celery, scallions, pepper, corn, walnuts and shredded lettuce. Add to the lettuce-lined salad bowl and chill.

Core the apple, chop it into cubes and mix with lemon juice to prevent it from browning. Add it to the salad. Cut the tomato into wedges and place them around the edge of the bowl. Sprinkle with parsley and serve.

SERVES 4

RUSSIAN RED CABBAGE SALAD

6 cups shredded red cabbage

1 cinnamon stick

1 cup apple cider vinegar

1 green apple

2 tablespoons lemon juice

1 cup sliced mushrooms

½ cup grated onion

3 tablespoons yogurt

freshly ground black pepper

¼ teaspoon prepared mustard

Put the cabbage in a bowl with the cinnamon stick. Heat the vinegar, pour it over the cabbage, cover the bowl and allow to stand until cold. Drain off the liquid and remove the cinnamon stick.

Peel, core and cut the apples into cubes, then sprinkle with 1 tablespoon of lemon juice to prevent browning. Combine the cabbage, apple, mushrooms and onion in a salad bowl.

Mix the remaining lemon juice, yogurt, pepper and mustard together and pour over the salad just before serving.

SERVES 4

POTATO NUT SALAD

½ pound new potatoes

1 tablespoon olive oil

2 stalks celery, chopped

1 green apple

1 tablespoon lemon juice

¼ cup pine nuts

¼ cup chopped scallions

¼ cup chopped red pepper

½ cup yogurt

1 tablespoon tomato purée

freshly ground black pepper

¼ teaspoon dry mustard

1 tablespoon pine nuts, toasted

Boil the potatoes in their jackets until tender. Cool, peel and chop into small cubes. Pour the oil over them and mix gently. Add the celery to the potatoes. Core the unpeeled apple and chop it into small cubes. Toss in lemon juice to prevent browning, then add to potatoes.

Place the potato mixture into a salad bowl and stir in the pine nuts, scallions and pepper. Cover and chill while you make the dressing.

Beat together the yogurt, tomato purée, pepper and mustard. Pour over the salad, mix well and serve garnished with toasted pine nuts.

SERVES 4

SPRINGTIME SALAD

3 cups cauliflower florets

1 avocado

juice 1 lemon

1 cup asparagus pieces

1 head lettuce

¼ cup chopped scallions

1 tablespoon olive oil

4 tablespoons tarragon vinegar

1 teaspoon chopped fresh parsley

freshly ground black pepper

¼ teaspoon prepared mustard

toasted sesame seeds, to garnish

Steam cauliflower until tender but still crisp. Refresh under cold water and pat dry. Halve the avocado, peel and pit. Cut the flesh into cubes and sprinkle with lemon juice to prevent browning.

Cover asparagus pieces with boiling water, cook for 5 minutes, refresh under cold water and pat dry. Wash and shred the lettuce.

Combine cauliflower, avocado, asparagus and scallions and chill.

Blend the oil, vinegar, parsley, pepper and mustard. Pour it over the salad, toss and serve on a bed of lettuce leaves garnished with toasted sesame seeds.

SERVES 4

Springtime Salad

ORANGE AND AVOCADO SALAD

4 oranges, chilled
1 large avocado
juice of 1–2 limes
2 teaspoons Dijon mustard
watercress sprigs, to garnish

Peel the oranges and carefully remove all the white pith. With a very sharp knife, section each orange and remove pips, being careful to retain any juices that squeeze out. Arrange the orange sections on 4 plates.

Slice the avocado into equal pieces. Whisk the lime juice, adding mustard and a little orange juice. Arrange the avocado on each plate with the orange slices. Drizzle the lime dressing over the avocado and orange and serve topped with sprigs of watercress.

SERVES 4

CURRIED BROWN RICE SALAD

3 cups cooked brown rice
½ cup diced red pepper
½ cup canned corn, drained
¼ cup chopped scallions
freshly ground black pepper
¼ cup chopped celery
3 tablespoons salad oil
1½ tablespoons tarragon vinegar
1½ teaspoons chopped fresh parsley
1 tablespoon curry powder

Mix the rice, pepper, corn, scallions, pepper and celery in a bowl. Blend oil, vinegar, parsley and curry powder. Pour over the salad. Toss well and serve.

SERVES 4–6

Orange and Avocado Salad

FARMHOUSE SALAD

Two 6-ounce packages cream cheese
1 cup grated Cheddar cheese
¼ cup cream
¼ cup chopped red pepper
¼ cup chopped scallions
¼ cup pine nuts
3 teaspoons lemon juice
¼ teaspoon paprika
1 head lettuce
3 tomatoes
1½ tablespoons chopped chives

Beat the cream cheese until smooth, add Cheddar and cream and mix until well blended. Stir in the pepper, scallions, pine nuts, lemon juice and paprika. Spread the mixture in a small freezer tray and chill until firm.

Wash and shred the lettuce and cut the tomatoes into wedges. Place the lettuce on a serving dish and arrange the tomato wedges on top.

Remove the cheese from the tray, cut into cubes and place them on the salad. Sprinkle with chives and serve.

SERVES 4

ORANGE AND SPINACH SALAD

½ bunch spinach

4 scallions, chopped

¼ cup toasted sliced almonds

2 oranges, peeled and sectioned

3 tablespoons olive oil

1¼ tablespoons vinegar

1¼ tablespoons lemon juice

freshly ground black pepper

pinch of dry mustard

Wash the spinach and remove stalks. Shred it and drain in a colander.

Mix together the spinach, scallions and almonds and place on a serving dish. Arrange the sliced oranges over the spinach.

Combine the oil, vinegar, lemon juice, pepper and mustard and pour it over the salad. Chill for 1 hour before serving.

SERVES 4

ZUCCHINI AND CHEESE SALAD

½ pound zucchini

4 celery stalks, cut in strips

1 cup diced Gruyère cheese

12 small radishes, cut in half

¼ cup walnuts, roughly chopped

1 teaspoon Dijon mustard

5 tablespoons mayonnaise

juice ½ lemon

1 Belgian endive cut into rings, to garnish

Cut zucchini diagonally into ½-inch slices. Blanch in boiling, salted water for 1 minute. Drain and plunge into iced water. Pat dry on paper towels.

Orange and Spinach Salad (above) and Zucchini and Cheese Salad

Mix zucchini with celery, cheese, radishes and walnuts. Whisk the mustard into the mayonnaise and add lemon juice. Drizzle the mayonnaise mixture onto the salad and serve garnished with endive.

SERVES 4-6

MACARONI AND ZUCCHINI SALAD

½ pound zucchini

salt

1 cup sliced mushrooms

1 cup cooked whole wheat macaroni

¾ cup cream

¼ cup crunchy peanut butter

½ cup mayonnaise

1 tablespoon honey

1 tablespoon white wine vinegar

1 tablespoon lemon juice

½ cup roasted peanuts

Wash and slice the zucchini. Sprinkle with salt and let stand for 30 minutes. Rinse under cold water and pat dry. Combine the zucchini, mushrooms and macaroni in a salad bowl and chill while you prepare the dressing.

Place all the remaining ingredients except the peanuts in a blender and whip until smooth but not too thick. Coat the salad lightly with the dressing. Chill well and serve garnished with roasted peanuts. Any leftover dressing will keep for 2 days in the refrigerator.

SERVES 4-6

BEAN SALAD

½ cup cooked kidney beans

½ cup cooked soybeans

½ cup cooked lima beans

1 cup cooked green beans

1 tablespoon chopped parsley

1 cup shredded cabbage

½ cup chopped onion

2 tablespoons olive oil

4 tablespoons white wine vinegar

freshly ground black pepper

Mix together the beans, parsley, cabbage and onion in a salad bowl. Beat the oil into the vinegar and add pepper. Pour over salad and chill well before serving.

SERVES 4

WALDORF SALAD WITH PEAS

4 green apples

juice 2 lemons

½ head lettuce, shredded

1 cup cooked peas

½ cup chopped celery

½ cup chopped walnuts

3 tablespoons olive oil

4 tablespoons white wine vinegar

¼ teaspoon prepared mustard

freshly ground black pepper

Peel, core and dice the apples and sprinkle with lemon juice to prevent browning.

Wash and shred the lettuce and combine with the apples, peas, celery and walnuts in a salad bowl.

Mix together the oil, vinegar, mustard and pepper and pour over the salad. Toss and serve.

SERVES 4

FRUIT AND NUT SALAD

2 grapefruits, peeled and
   sectioned

2 oranges, peeled and sectioned

1 cup chopped fresh pineapple

1 large green apple, chopped

1 tablespoon lemon juice

½ cup stuffed olives

½ lettuce

¼ cup toasted almonds

¼ cup chopped walnuts

1 tablespoon olive oil

Fruit and Nut Salad

2 tablespoons white wine vinegar

freshly ground black pepper

1 tablespoon chopped chives

Mix together the grapefruit, oranges
and pineapple in a bowl and chill.
Toss the apples in lemon juice to
prevent browning and add to other
fruit with the olives.

Wash the lettuce, place the leaves on
a serving dish and spoon the fruit
mixture on top. Sprinkle with nuts.

Combine the oil, vinegar, pepper
and chives and pour over the salad
just before serving.

SERVES 4

WARM BEET SALAD

2 pounds beets

5 tablespoons good salad oil

1 tablespoon white wine vinegar

freshly ground black pepper

1 tablespoon fennel, grated

1 large onion, sliced

3 tablespoons butter

chives, to garnish

Preheat oven to 350°F. Trim the
beets, wrap each one in foil and bake
for an hour or until they are tender
when tested with a toothpick. Cool
until you can handle them and peel
off the skins. Cut beets into strips.
Mix together the oil, vinegar and
pepper and pour over the beets. You
may not need all of it. Sprinkle with
fennel. Fry the onion in the butter
until it is golden. Pour over the beet
and mix gently. Garnish with chives.

SERVES 6–8

SICILIAN FENNEL SALAD

1 clove garlic, crushed and chopped

1 cucumber, seeds removed and
   thinly sliced

1 onion, thinly sliced

1 peeled orange, in sections

4 tomatoes, sliced

1 bulb fennel, sliced

1 tablespoon oil

2 tablespoons lemon juice

freshly ground black pepper

½ teaspoon chopped basil

fresh basil, to garnish

Sprinkle the garlic over a serving
dish. Layer the prepared salad
vegetables on the platter and chill.
Mix together the oil, lemon juice,
pepper and basil, pour over the salad
and serve. Garnish with basil.

SERVES 4

*Warm Beet Salad (above) and Sicilian
Fennel Salad without tomato and onion*

Meatless Main Courses

*T*his chapter is the heart of the book. It will show those who have always eaten meat and two vegetables for dinner that there are a number of interesting alternatives, and it will give confirmed vegetarians a few new ideas.

The key to good nutrition is variety. This book is not a vegetarian cookbook, because it recognizes that most people still include meat in their diet. However, by cooking meatless main courses sometimes, you'll not only get out of your red meat rut, you'll naturally become healthier from the grains, legumes and vegetables that you may not have tried before.

TOFU SPINACH SOUFFLÉ

1 pound spinach

1 tablespoon oil or ghee

1 teaspoon dried thyme

1 teaspoon dried oregano

Two 6 to 8-ounce cakes fresh soft bean curd (tofu)

1 teaspoon kelp powder (available from Asian food stores)

6 tablespoons water

½ teaspoon freshly ground black pepper

4 egg whites

Remove the stalks from the spinach, wash well and chop the leaves very finely with a sharp knife or in a food processor.

Heat the oil in a pan and cook the spinach for 5 minutes with the thyme and oregano. Drain off excess liquid by pressing between two plates.

Blend tofu with kelp and water in a food processor or blender and add the pepper. Mix with the spinach and leave to cool.

Preheat oven to 375°F. Whisk the egg whites until they form stiff peaks and gently fold them through the spinach mixture. Lightly oil a soufflé dish and fill with the spinach mixture. Bake for 30–35 minutes until it is well risen and firm to the touch. Serve immediately.

SERVES 4

CRUNCHY NUT TERRINE

1 tablespoon oil

1½ cups chopped celery

1½ cups chopped onion

½ cup almond meal

1 cup chopped walnuts

1 cup toasted, chopped cashew nuts

¼ cup rolled oats

1 tablespoon sesame seeds

½ pound cottage cheese

3 eggs

¼ teaspoon freshly ground black pepper

1 teaspoon chopped fresh parsley

¼ teaspoon dried marjoram

Heat the oil and cook the celery and onion until golden. Drain and place in a bowl with all the remaining ingredients. Mix thoroughly.

Preheat the oven to 350°F. Grease two 6-cup loaf tins, and line with wax paper. Spoon half the mixture into each. Bake for 45 minutes and test for firmness by pressing lightly with your finger. If the terrine is not firm, bake for a further 5–8 minutes.

Leave to cool slightly in the pan, then turn out onto a plate and remove the paper. Serve hot or cold with a salad.

SERVES 8–10

SPICY BEAN SPROUTS

1 pound fresh bean sprouts

1½ tablespoons butter

1 teaspoon minced ginger root

1 teaspoon crushed garlic

2 onions, finely chopped

½ teaspoon turmeric

1 teaspoon cumin

¼ teaspoon paprika

1 teaspoon minced red chile

Wash the bean sprouts and drain well. Heat the butter in a frying pan and cook the ginger and garlic for 1 minute. Add the onions and cook for 3 minutes. Add the turmeric, cumin, paprika and chile and cook for 3 minutes. Stir in the sprouts, mix well and cook for 3 minutes.

SERVES 4

BRAISED CHINESE VEGETABLES

¼ cup oil

1 teaspoon grated ginger root

1 clove garlic, crushed

1 large onion, cut into eighths

1 carrot, sliced

1 stalk celery, sliced

1 red pepper, chopped

½ green pepper, chopped

2 small zucchini, sliced

½ pound snow peas, trimmed

1 cup water chestnuts, halved

1 cup bamboo shoots, sliced

1 cup broccoli florets

½ cup chicken stock

1 tablespoon soy sauce

½ teaspoon sesame oil

½ teaspoon chili sauce

3 tablespoons bean sprouts

scallions, shredded, to garnish

Heat the oil in a large frying pan or wok, add the ginger and garlic and cook until golden. Add the onion pieces, carrot and celery and stir over high heat. Add the peppers, zucchini, snow peas, water chestnuts, bamboo shoots and broccoli and toss gently until heated through.

Lower the heat, pour in the stock, soy sauce, sesame oil and chili sauce and stir until combined. Cover and heat gently for 2 minutes or until the vegetables are tender but still crisp. Add bean sprouts and serve garnished with shredded scallions.

SERVES 4

BEAN AND VEGETABLE TACOS

1 tablespoon oil

6 scallions, finely chopped

1 clove garlic, crushed

1 carrot, finely chopped

1 stalk celery, finely chopped

One 15-ounce can red kidney beans

2 cups fresh or canned tomato sauce

chili sauce, to taste

8 taco shells

Cheddar cheese, grated

2 tomatoes, diced

lettuce leaves, finely shredded

Heat the oil in a frying pan and add the scallions, garlic, carrot and celery. Stir over low heat for 5 minutes, then add the kidney beans and mash with the back of a wooden spoon. Add the tomato sauce and chili sauce, reduce the heat and simmer for 10 minutes. If the mixture starts to thicken too much, add a little water.

Preheat oven to 350°F. Place the taco shells upside down on the rungs of the oven rack and heat for 8–10 minutes. Spoon some of the bean mixture into each taco shell, top with grated cheese, then diced tomato and shredded lettuce.

SERVES 4

ONION AND NUT PIE

⅔ cup finely diced carrots

2 pounds onions, thinly sliced

½ pound mushrooms, sliced

6 cabbage leaves

2 eggs

1 tablespoon powdered milk

½ cup water

¼ teaspoon dried thyme

2 tablespoons pine nuts

2 tablespoons hazelnuts

2 tablespoons cashews

3 tablespoons margarine

2 cups soft brown breadcrumbs

1 teaspoon yeast extract (e.g. Marmite)

1 teaspoon chopped chives

1 teaspoon chopped parsley

Place the carrots in a large saucepan with a little water and cook for 5 minutes. Drain off the water and add the onions to the pan. Cover and cook over gentle heat for 5 minutes, stirring often to prevent them from sticking or browning. Add the mushrooms and cook for a further minute. Do not allow them to brown.

Remove the hard stems from the cabbage leaves and plunge them into boiling water for 4 minutes. Remove, rinse under cold water and pat dry. Line a greased 8-inch (12-cup) springform pan with cabbage leaves, allowing the leaves to hang over the edge of the tin.

Mix together the eggs, powdered milk, water and thyme and stir into the onion mixture. Spoon the filling evenly into the prepared springform pan and trim the cabbage leaves to be level with the top of the filling.

Grind all the nuts in a blender and mix with the remaining ingredients. Sprinkle this topping over the onion filling.

Preheat oven to 400°F. Place the cake tin in a baking dish half-filled with cold water and bake 1 hour. Remove the pan from the water and allow to stand for 5 minutes before opening the sides of the tin. Serve warm, in slices.

SERVES 6

BAKED VEGETABLE RING WITH TOMATO FILLING

2 onions, chopped

2 cloves garlic, chopped

1 tablespoon oil

1 bunch spinach

2 cups cottage cheese

2 cups cooked soybeans

½ cup chopped walnuts

½ cup golden raisins

¼ cup tomato paste

¼ cup grated carrot

¼ teaspoon dried dill

freshly ground black pepper

FRESH TOMATO FILLING

2 tomatoes, peeled and chopped

¼ cup chopped onion

1 tablespoon chopped fresh mint

1 tablespoon lemon juice

pinch of cayenne

Fry the onions and garlic in oil until they are soft but not brown. Wash the spinach and remove the stalks. Steam until just tender, then chop it finely and drain in a colander. When cool enough to handle, press out all liquid. Combine the spinach with the cooked onion and all remaining ingredients.

Preheat oven to 350°F. Grease a ring mold and line it with wax paper. Spoon in the spinach mixture and press down firmly. Cover the mold with foil and bake for 45 minutes or until firm when tested with your finger. (Remove the foil after 25 minutes.) Allow to stand for 10 minutes before turning out onto a serving dish.

To make the filling, mix the tomatoes with the onion, mint, lemon juice and cayenne. Spoon into the center of the vegetable ring and serve.

SERVES 4–6

HOT RICE SALAD

1 cup cooked brown rice

3 tablespoons butter

1 onion, chopped

¼ cup chopped snow peas

¼ cup chopped red pepper

1 zucchini, sliced

2 spinach leaves, finely chopped

red pepper, cut in strips, to garnish

DRESSING

2 hard-boiled eggs, chopped

freshly ground black pepper

¼ teaspoon paprika

½ cup sour crĪeam

Keep the cooked rice hot in a colander over hot water. Melt the butter in a frying pan and add the onion, snow peas, pepper and zucchini. Cook for 5 minutes and

Hot Rice Salad

mix with the hot rice. Add the spinach to the rice.

To make the dressing, place the chopped eggs in a saucepan with the pepper, paprika and sour cream. Heat but do not boil. Place the salad in a serving bowl and pour over the sour cream dressing. Garnish with strips of red pepper.

SERVES 4

Spanish Omelet (above) and Cashew Nut Roast

CASHEW NUT ROAST

oil

1–2 tablespoons dried breadcrumbs

5½ tablespoons butter

1 onion, finely chopped

¼ pound mushrooms, sliced

¼ teaspoon dried marjoram

1⅓ cups rolled oats

1⅓ cups milk

1 egg, beaten

freshly ground black pepper

½ pound raw unsalted cashew nuts, very finely chopped

fresh marjoram, to garnish

Preheat oven to 350°F. Lightly oil a 6-cup loaf pan and coat with breadcrumbs. Melt the butter and sauté the onion and mushrooms for 2 minutes. Add the marjoram and rolled oats and gradually add the milk, stirring continuously. Cool slightly, then stir in the egg and nuts. Season to taste. The mixture should be a soft dropping consistency.

Pour it into the pan and smooth over the top with a spatula. Bake for 1¼ hours. Garnish with marjoram.

SERVES 6

ORIENTAL BROWN RICE

1¼ cups long grain brown rice

4 tablespoons oil

16 scallions, chopped

1 clove garlic, crushed

3 tablespoons grated ginger

4 sticks celery, diced

One 6-ounce can water chestnuts, sliced

1 pound bean sprouts

4 tablespoons chopped parsley

1 teaspoon dried oregano

½ teaspoon dried basil

½ cup sunflower seeds

½ cup honey

⅓ cup soy sauce

1 tablespoon lemon juice

Two 6-ounce cans mandarin oranges, drained

Cook the rice until tender. Heat the oil in a wok or large frying pan and add the scallions, garlic and ginger. Sauté for 1 minute. Add the celery, water chestnuts, bean sprouts and parsley and stir-fry for 1 minute. Add the herbs and sunflower seeds.

Mix together the honey, soy sauce and lemon juice and stir into the vegetables. Add the rice and oranges and heat through gently.

SERVES 6

MUGHAL VEGETABLES

3 tablespoons oil

2 onions, sliced

seeds from 6 cardamom pods

One 2-inch stick cinnamon, broken in pieces

2 tablespoons poppy seeds

¾ teaspoon chili powder

¼ teaspoon ground cloves

½ pound cauliflower florets

½ pound zucchini, sliced

1 cup carrots, sliced

⅓ pound green beans, sliced

¼ pound mushrooms, sliced

⅓ cup desiccated coconut

¼ cup slivered almonds

¼ cup pistachio nuts (optional)

2 cups beef stock

⅔ cup sour cream

2 teaspoons lemon juice

Heat the oil in a large saucepan and sauté the onions until they are soft but not brown. Add spices, vegetables, nuts and stock and season to taste. Bring to the boil, cover and simmer for 15 minutes or until the vegetables are tender.

Using a slotted spoon, transfer the vegetables to a serving dish and keep them warm. Add sour cream and lemon juice to the liquid in the pan, reheat and spoon over the vegetables.

SERVES 4

TOMATO RELISH

4 under-ripe tomatoes, peeled and chopped

1 onion, chopped

1 stalk celery, chopped

¼ cup horseradish cream

1 teaspoon Dijon mustard

1 tablespoon brown sugar

1 cup malt vinegar

To make the tomato relish, place all the ingredients in a saucepan, cover and simmer for 45 minutes. Spoon the mixture into sterilized warm jars, seal and store in the refrigerator.

SPANISH OMELET

3 tablespoons olive oil

1 large peeled potato, diced

1 large onion, finely chopped

5 eggs

freshly ground black pepper

Heat the oil in a large frying pan. Sauté the potato and onion, stirring occasionally, until both are cooked but not brown. Whisk the eggs with pepper and pour it into the pan, spreading evenly. Cover the pan, lower the heat and allow the omelet to cook for about 10 minutes.

Place a plate of a similar size to your frying pan over the top of it and invert the omelet on it. Slide it immediately back into the pan and allow the other side to brown. It will be thick and golden in color when it is ready.

SERVES 4

CHEESY CARROT RING

3 tablespoons butter

2 pounds young carrots, finely chopped

freshly ground black pepper

1 cup chicken or vegetable stock

¼ pound button mushrooms, chopped

1 teaspoon olive oil

2 eggs, beaten

¼ cup grated Edam cheese

1 teaspoon chopped fresh dill

Heat the butter in a pan, add the carrots and brown lightly. Add pepper and stock, cover the pan and simmer for 30 minutes. Sauté the mushrooms in olive oil for 3 minutes, then drain.

Preheat oven to 400°F. Combine carrots and mushrooms in a bowl, with eggs, cheese and dill. Grease a ring mold and line with wax paper. Spoon the mixture into the mold and press down firmly. Cover with foil and place in a baking dish with 1 inch of water.

Bake for 20 minutes, reduce heat to 350°F and bake for a further 20 minutes. Allow to stand for 10 minutes before turning out onto a serving dish.

SERVES 6

EGGPLANT AND WALNUT PUFF

1 pound eggplant

3 tablespoons butter

2 tablespoons flour

1 cup milk

4 eggs, separated

2 tablespoons chopped walnuts

pinch of grated nutmeg

freshly ground black pepper

Preheat the oven to 400°F. Bake the whole eggplant for 30 minutes or until pulp is soft. Remove from oven and reduce oven heat to 375°F. Meanwhile, melt the butter in a pan, stir in the flour and cook for 1 minute. Gradually add the milk, stirring continuously until thick and smooth. Remove the sauce from the heat. Lightly beat the egg yolks and add to the sauce with the walnuts, nutmeg and pepper.

Split the eggplant, scrape out the pulp, mash well and stir it into the sauce. Beat the egg whites until stiff and fold them into the sauce.

Pour the mixture into an oiled soufflé dish and bake for 45 minutes. Serve immediately.

SERVES 4

CABBAGE CAKE

4 large green cabbage leaves

3 cups chopped green vegetables (spinach, sorrel, Chinese cabbage, leeks, onions, scallions)

1 egg

1 egg white

2 tablespoons yogurt

2 tablespoons cottage cheese

1 tablespoon mixed fresh herbs (chives, parsley, tarragon)

freshly ground black pepper

Remove the thick stalks from the cabbage leaves and blanch for 2–3 minutes and drain. Blanch green vegetables for 2–3 minutes and drain.

Line a small ovenproof dish with the cabbage leaves, with the tips in the center and the base of the leaves hanging over the edge. The leaves must be large enough to cover the contents of the pan once the filling has been added.

Mix the blanched vegetables together and spoon onto the leaves. Combine the remaining ingredients, beating well. Pour the filling over the vegetables and enclose with the cabbage leaves.

Preheat oven to 350°F. Cover with foil and place in a baking dish half-filled with water. Bake for 1 hour. Remove and allow to rest for 15 minutes before turning it out of the dish. Slice and serve with fresh tomato sauce.

SERVES 4

ZYLDYK CASSEROLE

½ pound spinach

2 carrots, sliced

1 large zucchini, sliced

1 large onion, sliced

2 cups cauliflower florets

2 cups cabbage, shredded

2 tablespoons butter

1 tablespoon flour

3½ cups skim milk

2 cups Edam cheese, finely grated

1 tablespoon curry powder

2 slices whole wheat bread, crumbled

Remove stalks from the spinach and cook in a little water until tender. Place the carrots, zucchini, onion, cauliflower and cabbage in a saucepan and barely cover with water. Bring to the boil, then drain, reserving ⅔ cup of the liquid.

Place the vegetables in an ovenproof dish and arrange the spinach on top. Melt the butter, stir in the flour and cook for 1 minute. Gradually stir in the reserved vegetable liquid and the milk. Bring to the boil and simmer for 2 minutes, stirring continuously until thick. Remove from heat, add 1 cup cheese and all the curry powder and stir well. Spoon the sauce over the vegetables.

Preheat oven to 375°F. Mix together the remaining cheese and the breadcrumbs and sprinkle over the dish. Bake for 30 minutes.

SERVES 4

VEGETABLE STRUDEL

2 carrots, thinly sliced

½ pound green beans

½ pound broccoli florets

1 leek

2 tablespoons butter

4 medium-sized mushrooms, sliced

1 stalk celery, finely chopped

¼ pound bean sprouts

5 sheets filo pastry

5 tablespoons butter, melted

1½ cups grated Cheddar cheese

3 cups fresh breadcrumbs

freshly ground black pepper

1 tablespoon finely chopped fresh basil

fresh chervil, to garnish

carrot, cut in matchsticks, to garnish

Blanch the carrots for 2 minutes, drain and set aside. Trim and slice the beans and cook for 3 minutes in boiling water, drain and set aside. Blanch broccoli florets for 3 minutes, drain and set aside.

Wash the leek well and slice the white part very finely. Melt the butter and cook the leek over low heat until it is soft. Add the mushrooms to the pan. Cook for 1 minute, then add the celery and cook for 1 minute. Add the bean sprouts and the reserved vegetables and toss well. Allow to cool.

Preheat oven to 375°F. Brush 5 sheets of filo pastry with melted butter and place them one on top of the other. Mix together the cheese

and breadcrumbs and sprinkle half over the top layer of pastry. Add the vegetables in a layer and sprinkle with the remaining cheese and crumbs. Season with pepper and basil.

Roll up the pastry, seal and brush with melted butter. Bake for 35 minutes. Before serving, decorate with chervil and carrot sticks.

SERVES 6

Vegetable Strudel

BROAD BEAN CASSEROLE

3 cups shelled broad beans (about 3 pounds)

1½ tablespoons butter

1 bay leaf

1 cup tomato relish (see p. 55)

pinch of dried basil

Preheat oven to 350°F. Cook the broad beans in a small amount of boiling water until they are just tender. Drain and place in a casserole dish with all the other ingredients. Cover and bake for 15 minutes. Remove cover and continue baking for another 15 minutes.

SERVES 4

SPINACH TARTS

PASTRY

1¼ cups flour

¼ teaspoon salt

4 tablespoons butter, diced

3 tablespoons vegetable
shortening, diced

2 tablespoons iced water

FILLING

3 tablespoons butter

3 tablespoons chopped scallions

1½ cups spinach, cooked and
drained (or 1 package frozen
spinach)

dash nutmeg

freshly ground black pepper

½ pound cream cheese

4 eggs

½ cup cream

fresh watercress, to garnish

cherry tomatoes, to garnish

To make the pastry, mix together the flour and the salt. Using your fingertips, rub the butter and shortening into the flour until the mixture resembles coarse breadcrumbs. Add water and knead lightly. Form the dough into a ball, dust with flour, wrap in wax paper and chill for 1 hour.

Roll the dough thinly and line 6 small tart pans. Prick the base of the shells and chill for 1 hour.

Spinach Tarts

To make the filling, melt the butter in a pan over medium heat and add the scallions. When soft, add the spinach, nutmeg and pepper. Cook for 5 minutes. Place in a bowl and beat in the cream cheese. Separate the eggs, add 4 yolks, one at a time to the spinach. Add the cream. In another bowl, beat the egg whites until stiff and fold them into the spinach mixture.

Preheat oven to 400°F. Cover the base of the tarts with wax paper and dried beans or rice and bake for 15 minutes. Remove beans and paper and allow the pastry shells to cool.

Reduce oven heat to 350°F.

Fill shells with the spinach mixture, dot with butter and bake 15–20 minutes. Allow to cool before serving. Garnish with watercress and cherry tomatoes.

SERVES 6

INSTANT BEAN MEDLEY

1 tablespoon oil

1 onion, chopped

1 red pepper, chopped

One 1-pound can soybeans

One 1-pound can red kidney beans

One 1-pound can pink or white beans

One 11-can lima beans

One 8-ounce can small mushrooms

One 1-pound can corn

One 14-ounce can asparagus pieces

One 28-ounce can whole tomatoes

freshly ground black pepper

¾ teaspoon chili powder

1 tablespoon chopped chives

1 cup grated Cheddar cheese

½ cup soft breadcrumbs

Preheat oven to 375°F. Sauté the onion and pepper in oil until the onion is soft but not brown. Drain all the cans of their liquid and mix together all the ingredients except the cheese and breadcrumbs. Spoon into a greased casserole.

Mix together the cheese and breadcrumbs and sprinkle on top. Bake for 20 minutes, then brown the top before serving.

SERVES 4–6

STIR-FRY TOFU

2 cups boiling water

1 cup bean sprouts

1 large cake firm bean curd (tofu)

¼ cup vegetable oil

1 clove garlic, crushed

1 teaspoon grated fresh ginger root

4 scallions, cut in 1-inch lengths

6 small mushrooms, sliced

½ red pepper cut in thin strips

½ teaspoon soy sauce

Pour boiling water over the bean sprouts, leave to stand for 2 minutes, then drain. Rinse the tofu in hot water, drain on paper towels and cut into 1-inch cubes.

Heat the oil in a frying pan and add the garlic, ginger, scallions, mushrooms and pepper. Cook for about 6 minutes, stirring from time to time. Add all the remaining ingredients, heat through and serve immediately.

SERVES 2

OKRA CASSEROLE

1 eggplant

salt

2 carrots, sliced

2 potatoes, peeled and sliced

2 onions, sliced

¼ cup olive oil

4 zucchini, sliced

4 tomatoes, sliced

2 cups okra, canned or fresh

¼ cup chopped fresh parsley

2 teaspoons dried oregano

freshly ground black pepper

¼ teaspoon nutmeg

Cut eggplant into slices, sprinkle with salt and let stand for

30 minutes. Simmer the carrots and potatoes in water for 5 minutes. Drain and refresh under cold water. Rinse the eggplant and pat dry.

Heat the oil and sauté the onions until soft but not brown. Remove with a slotted spoon and add the eggplant. Fry until golden on both sides. Trim the okra.

Preheat the oven to 375°F. In a deep casserole dish, layer all the vegetables, sprinkling each layer with a little parsley, oregano, pepper and nutmeg. Cover the casserole and bake for 1 hour or until tender.

SERVES 6

BARLEY VEGETABLE CASSEROLE

⅔ cup pearl barley

2½ cups chicken stock

1 tablespoon oil

1 clove garlic, crushed

1 onion, chopped

2 sticks celery, chopped

2 carrots, finely diced

2 tablespoons tomato paste

1 cup frozen peas

Soak the barley overnight in the stock. Bring to the boil and simmer for 1 hour. Drain the barley and reserve the liquid.

Heat the oil and sauté the garlic, onion, celery and carrots for 8 minutes, stirring occasionally to prevent them from browning. Add the tomato paste, cook for 1 minute, then add the barley stock and the peas. Simmer for 20 minutes, until the vegetables are tender and the liquid has almost evaporated. Add the barley and reheat.

SERVES 4

VEGETABLE CURRY

⅓ cup oil

2 teaspoons cumin

½ teaspoon turmeric

¼ teaspoon chili powder

2 large onions, chopped

2 cloves garlic, crushed

small piece of ginger root, grated

2 large tomatoes, peeled and chopped

4 potatoes, quartered

¼ head cauliflower, cut into florets

3–4 zucchini, sliced

½ eggplant, diced

1 cup frozen peas

½ cup water

Heat the oil and stir in the cumin, turmeric and chili powder. Add the onions, garlic and ginger and sauté, stirring until the onions are soft but not brown. Add all the vegetables except the peas and sauté, stirring, for 5 minutes.

Add the water, cover and simmer over low heat for 20 minutes. Add the peas and simmer 5 minutes more. Most of the moisture should be absorbed during cooking.

SERVES 4

RIBBON BEAN BAKE

1 tablespoon olive oil

1 onion, chopped

1 clove garlic, finely chopped

¼ cup chopped celery

1 tablespoon chili sauce

½ cup tomato purée

¼ cup tomato paste

¼ cup red wine

freshly ground black pepper

¼ teaspoon dried oregano

¼ teaspoon dried basil

½ cup cooked broad beans

½ cup cooked red kidney beans

1 cup cooked soybeans

½ cup cooked lima beans

½ cup cooked chick peas

½ pound ricotta cheese

½ pound mozzarella cheese, thinly sliced

grated Parmesan cheese

Heat the oil and cook the onion, garlic and celery for 5 minutes. Add the chili sauce, tomato purée and paste, wine, pepper, oregano and basil and simmer for 25 minutes.

Preheat oven to 375°F. Place all the beans and peas in a bowl and mix together. Beat the ricotta cheese in a bowl until smooth.

Place one-third of the tomato sauce in the bottom of a medium-sized casserole. Spoon in one-third of the bean mixture and spread one-third of the ricotta over the beans. Place one-third of the mozzarella sliced on the ricotta.

Repeat layers twice and sprinkle the finished casserole with Parmesan cheese. Cover and bake for 30 minutes. Remove lid and bake for 10 minutes more to brown the top.

SERVES 4–6

BOLIVIAN BEAN STEW

1 cup broad beans

1 cup chick peas

chicken stock

1 cup lentils

1 green pepper, roughly chopped

1 red pepper, roughly chopped

4 sticks celery, thickly sliced

2 carrots, chopped

½ pound tomatoes, peeled

One 11-ounce can whole kernel corn, drained

2 tablespoons tomato paste

bouquet garni

Soak the beans and chick peas overnight in water to cover. Drain and measure liquid, adding chicken stock to make up to 3 cups.

Place all the ingredients in a saucepan and bring to the boil very slowly — it should take about 30 minutes — then simmer for 1–1½ hours or until the beans and chick peas are tender. Remove the bouquet garni and season to taste.

SERVES 6

HUNGARIAN BEAN AND VEGETABLE LOAF

¾ pound (1½ cups) cranberry beans

¾ pound (1½ cups) soybeans

1 bay leaf

2 onions, finely chopped

4 cloves garlic, crushed

1 pepper, seeded and diced

2 eggs, beaten

1 tablespoon oil

2 slices stale whole wheat bread, crumbed

1 tablespoon chopped fresh parsley

freshly ground black pepper

1 pound spinach

¼ pound roasted unsalted peanuts

¼ pound button mushrooms

1–2 chiles, seeded and chopped

One 2-ounce can green peppercorns

1–2 tablespoons paprika

Soak the beans overnight in water to cover. Add the bay leaf, bring to the boil and simmer for 1 hour or until tender. Purée the beans in a blender

with a little of the cooking liquid. Add the onions, garlic, pepper, eggs, oil, breadcrumbs and parsley. Season to taste.

Wash the spinach well, remove the stalks and cook the leaves in a little water until just tender. Purée the spinach and press out excess liquid. Purée the peanuts and mushrooms and add to the spinach with the chiles and green peppercorns.

Preheat oven to 375°F. Place the bean mixture on a floured board and flatten to a thickness of roughly 1¾ inches with a rolling pin. Place the spinach mixture in the middle of the bean mixture and fold the bean mixture over to form a loaf. Sprinkle liberally with paprika then place it in a buttered ovenproof dish and bake for 1 hour. The loaf may be served hot or cold.

SERVES 6–8

VEGETABLE KEBABS

MARINADE

1 teaspoon garam masala

¼ teaspoon freshly ground black pepper

pinch of dried rosemary

1 tablespoon cumin

3 tablespoons sesame oil

juice of ½ lemon

KEBABS

4 button mushrooms

1 green or red pepper, cut into squares

4 small white onions

4 cherry tomatoes

½ eggplant, cut into 1-inch cubes

1 firm, ripe banana, cut into chunks

1 cake firm tofu, cut into ¾-inch cubes

4 spinach leaves, made into ¾-inch thick rolls

Vegetable Kebabs

4 cauliflower florets

1 apple, cut into cubes

parsley, for decoration

To make the marinade, place all the ingredients in a jar and shake well.

Arrange a selection of vegetables or fruit on skewers so that the cooking time of each is approximately the same. Brush over with the marinade and grill on a barbecue. Garnish with parsley.

SERVES 4

Main Courses

*I*ncluded here are recipes for fish, chicken and meat. It's not a very big chapter as the idea is to present some interesting, and for the most part light, main courses. The recipes are not rigidly 'healthy' — there's even a recipe for deep-fried shrimp and scallops — because following a healthy diet doesn't mean you have to miss out on all the things you enjoy. If you do that, you'll end up finding meal times a bore and going back to junk food.

So if you want to eat fried food occasionally, do it, but only occasionally. The problems arise if you eat it every day, or every second or third day.

FISH PIE

¾ pound firm fish fillets (cod, grouper, kingfish)

1½ cups milk

3 tablespoons butter

2 tablespoons flour

freshly ground black pepper

¼ cup finely chopped fresh parsley

1 hard-boiled egg, sliced

4 medium-sized potatoes, peeled

½ onion, very thinly sliced

1 teaspoon butter

1 tablespoon hot milk

2 tablespoons grated Parmesan cheese

Preheat oven to 350°F. Place the fish and ½ cup milk into an ovenproof dish. Cover and cook for 10–15 minutes. Remove fish from the pan, flake, and discard bones. Reserve the milk. Increase oven heat to 400°F.

In a saucepan, melt the butter and blend in the flour. Add the remaining milk plus the milk from the cooked fish, stir constantly and bring to the boil. Season with pepper and add the parsley. Return the fish to the casserole dish, top with the sliced egg and pour over the sauce.

Steam the potatoes and onion together for 20 minutes or until the potatoes are cooked. Mash both well with the butter and hot milk. Spread the mixture over the fish and sprinkle with cheese. Bake for 15 minutes.

SERVES 2

PROVENÇALE CHICKEN

8 chicken pieces

freshly ground black pepper

pinch of cinnamon

¼ cup oil

1 clove garlic, crushed

1 bunch scallions, chopped

1 green pepper, cut into strips

½ pound mushrooms

4 large tomatoes, peeled, seeded and chopped

½ cup dry white wine

⅔ cup tomato purée

bouquet garni

2 tablespoons fresh parsley, chopped

16 black olives

Season the chicken pieces with pepper and cinnamon. Heat the oil in a frying pan and brown the chicken pieces. Remove them with a slotted spoon and drain on paper towels.

Add the garlic, scallions, pepper and mushrooms to the pan and cook briefly until slightly wilted. Remove and drain. Add the tomatoes to the pan and cook for 2–3 minutes, then add the wine.

Return the vegetables to the pan with the tomato purée, bouquet garni and chicken pieces. Cook over low heat until the chicken is tender. Remove bouquet garni and serve chicken garnished with parsley and olives.

SERVES 4

APOLLO STEAK

4 rump steaks

1 tablespoon oil

SAUCE

2 tablespoons butter

1 large onion, sliced

1 small veal kidney, trimmed and separated (remove filament if desired)

2 tomatoes, peeled, seeded and chopped

1 green pepper, chopped

⅔ cup red wine

⅔ cup beef stock

pinch of oregano

To make the sauce, sauté the onion in butter for 5–8 minutes, until soft but not brown. Add the kidney,

tomatoes and pepper and simmer a further 5 minutes. Add the wine, stock and oregano, bring to the boil and simmer for 5 minutes.

Pan-fry the steaks to your taste. Spoon the sauce over and serve immediately.

SERVES 4

EGGPLANT KHORESH

1 large eggplant, diced

salt

¾ cup haricot beans, soaked overnight

2 onions, sliced

2 carrots, sliced

1 tablespoon oil

2 pounds breast of lamb cut in chunks

½ cup flour

freshly ground black pepper

2 cups beef stock

1 tablespoon tomato paste

2 sticks celery, chopped

Put the diced eggplant in a colander and sprinkle with salt. Cover with a weighted plate and set aside for 30 minutes. The salt will draw out the eggplant's bitter juices.

Drain the beans. Fry the onions and carrots in the oil until the onion is soft but not brown. Remove with a slotted spoon.

Lightly coat the lamb in seasoned flour and brown in the oil remaining in the pan. Rinse and dry the eggplant and add it with the beans, onions and carrots, stock, tomato paste and celery. Bring to the boil, cover and simmer for 2½ hours or until the meat and beans are tender.

If possible, chill overnight or for several hours, until the fat has set on top. Remove the fat and reheat the dish before serving.

SERVES 4–6

STIR-FRIED CHICKEN

2 teaspoons soy sauce

4 chicken breasts, cut into strips

2 tablespoons oil

1 large onion, quartered

1 teaspoon grated ginger root

1 clove garlic, crushed

2 sticks celery, sliced diagonally

1 red pepper, sliced

1 small carrot, sliced

1 can baby ears of corn, drained

¾ pound button mushrooms

2 teaspoons cornstarch

1 cup chicken stock

4 scallions, chopped

Sprinkle soy sauce over the chicken strips. Heat the oil in a wok and gently fry the chicken until cooked. Remove with a slotted spoon and drain. Add onion, ginger, garlic and celery to the wok and stir-fry over high heat. Add pepper, carrot and corn and stir-fry. Lower the heat and add the button mushrooms.

Blend the cornstarch with the stock and add to the wok with the chicken pieces and scallions. Increase the heat, stirring constantly, and cook until heated through.

Serves 6

GRILLED MARINATED FISH

2 thick snapper or porgy fillets, cut in 2-inch squares

MARINADE

1 tablespoon vegetable oil

2 tablespoons fruit chutney

1 teaspoon grated fresh ginger

1 teaspoon soy sauce

1 tablespoon white wine

Mix together all the ingredients for the marinade.

Arrange the fish in a flat dish and pour over the marinade. Marinate for 2 hours, turning the fish once or twice during this time.

Line a broiler pan with foil and arrange the fish pieces on it. Brush them with the marinade. Broil for 5 minutes, then brush with marinade again and broil a further 5 minutes or until the fish is cooked. It is not necessary to turn the fish.

SERVES 2

Stir-fried Chicken

CHICKEN HAWAIIAN

1½ cups pineapple juice

1 tablespoon finely chopped onion

1 teaspoon grated fresh ginger root

1 clove garlic, crushed

2 tablespoons fruit chutney

1 tablespoon soy sauce

1 frying chicken (about 3 pounds), quartered and skinned

fresh pineapple slices, to garnish

Combine pineapple juice, onion, ginger, garlic, chutney and soy sauce to make a marinade.

Line a baking dish with foil and place the chicken pieces on it. Pour over the marinade and let sit for 2 hours.

Preheat oven to 375°F. Bake the chicken in the marinade for three-quarters of an hour, basting occasionally. When chicken is cooked, remove and serve with fresh pineapple slices.

SERVES 4

LAMB AND NUT KORMA

⅓ cup raw cashew nuts

3 dried chiles

2 teaspoons ground coriander

1 teaspoon ground ginger

1 teaspoon cumin

½ teaspoon cinnamon

pinch of ground cardamom

pinch of ground cloves

2 cloves garlic, crushed

⅔ cup water

2 onions, chopped

3 tablespoons butter or ghee

⅔ cup yogurt

1½ pounds lean lamb (leg), diced

grated rind of ½ lemon

2 teaspoons lemon juice

½ teaspoon turmeric

Grind the nuts and chiles together. If using a food processor, a little water may be needed. Mix together the coriander, ginger, cumin, cinnamon, cardamom, cloves and garlic. Add the nut mixture and water and blend to a smooth paste.

Sauté the onions in the butter over low heat until soft but not brown. Stir in the spice and nut paste and add the yogurt. Fry over gentle heat until the oil separates.

Add the lamb, toss well in the mixture and add the lemon rind, lemon juice and the turmeric. Bring to the boil, cover and simmer for 1 hour.

SERVES 4

BROILED KINGFISH STEAKS

4 whole kingfish steaks

1 teaspoon Dijon mustard

juice of 1 lemon

freshly ground black pepper

3 tablespoons butter

fresh coriander, to garnish

Heat the broiler. Smear mustard over the steaks. Place the fish on foil, sprinkle with lemon juice, season lightly and dot with knobs of butter.

Broil until fish flakes when tested. Serve garnished with fresh coriander.

SERVES 4

FISH WITH PEANUT SAUCE

2 pounds fish fillets (grouper, cod), skinned

2 tablespoons flour

2 tablespoons oil

2 tablespoons butter

2 tablespoons smooth peanut butter

1 tablespoon honey

1 tablespoon soy sauce

1 tablespoon vinegar

⅔ cup flat light beer

pinch of chili powder

½ cup raw peanuts

1 lemon, cut into wedges

Divide the fish into 4 pieces. Coat each piece lightly with flour. Heat the oil and butter together and fry the fish for 5 minutes on each side.

Place all the remaining ingredients except the peanuts and lemon wedges in a pan and boil until the mixture has reduced by half. Add the peanuts and simmer over low heat for 3 minutes.

Put the fish on a heated serving dish and spoon over the sauce. Serve with lemon wedges.

SERVES 4

BAKED FISH CASSEROLE

One ½-pound piece frozen white fish, cut in 2 pieces

2 tablespoons lemon juice

freshly ground black pepper

1 tablespoon finely chopped fresh parsley

½ onion, thinly sliced

pinch of dried dill

2 tablespoons dry breadcrumbs

1 tablespoon vegetable oil

Preheat oven to 375°F. Place frozen fish in a baking dish. Sprinkle over lemon juice, ground pepper, parsley, onion slices and dill. Bake for 15 minutes. Remove from oven and increase heat.

Mix breadcrumbs and oil together and spread lightly over the casserole. Brown in the oven for an additional 5 minutes.

SERVES 2

CURRIED FISH RISOTTO

1 large onion, chopped

2 tablespoons oil

1 tablespoon flour

2–3 tablespoons curry powder

2½ cups chicken stock

1 cup long grain rice

1 green pepper, sliced

1 small Granny Smith apple, peeled, cored and chopped

1 tablespoon golden raisins

freshly ground black pepper

1½ pounds firm white fish, skinned and boned

Sauté the onion in the oil until soft but not brown. Stir in the flour and curry powder and cook for 1 minute. Add the stock, rice, pepper, apple and golden raisins and season to taste. Cover the pan and simmer for 15 minutes, stirring occasionally.

Cut the fish into bite-sized pieces, add to the curry and simmer for 5 minutes, until rice and fish are cooked.

SERVES 4

CHICKEN CHASSEUR

½ chicken, cut into 4 pieces

freshly ground black pepper

½ onion, chopped

½ apple, chopped

¼ pound fresh mushrooms, sliced

1 clove garlic, chopped

½ cup white wine

1 cup prepared pasta sauce

Preheat oven to 400°F. Remove the skin from the chicken pieces and place the chicken in a casserole. Sprinkle with pepper and brown in the oven for 10 minutes. Remove. Lower heat to 350°F. Skim off fat

carefully, and arrange onion, apple, mushrooms and garlic around chicken. Pour in wine and tomato sauce and bake for 40 minutes.

SERVES 2

SPICY PEANUT ROAST CHICKEN

1 teaspoon paprika

1 teaspoon ground ginger

pinch of cayenne

3 tablespoons oil

3 cups raw peanuts

1 chicken (about 3 pounds)

¼ pound (1 stick) butter

3–4 slices whole wheat bread

2 tablespoons rum

Preheat oven to 350°F. Mix together paprika, ginger, cayenne and oil. Grind 1 cup of the peanuts in a food processor and add half of it to the oil and spices. Truss the chicken for roasting and coat with the mixture. Bake for 1½ hours or until tender.

Mix the remaining ground peanuts with half the butter. Toast the bread, spread it with the peanut butter, place on a baking sheet and bake for 5–10 minutes, or until the topping is brown and bubbling. Sauté the remaining 2 cups of peanuts in the rest of the butter until they are pale golden.

To serve, cut the toast in half and arrange around the chicken on a hot serving dish. Sprinkle over the peanuts, heat the rum carefully, pour it over the chicken and set alight.

SERVES 6

STEAMED TROUT WITH LIME BUTTER

2 small fresh trout, washed and dried

juice 2 limes

*pinch of **herbes de Provence** (dried thyme, rosemary, marjoram and oregano)*

freshly ground black pepper

LIME BUTTER

4 tablespoons butter

grated zest and juice of ½ lime

To make lime butter, beat the butter with a wooden spoon or in a food

Steamed Trout with Lime Butter

processor until smooth. Thoroughly beat in lime zest and juice, transfer the butter to a decorative serving bowl and refrigerate until needed.

Cut out two 12-inch squares of aluminum foil. Place trout on the foil and put 1 teaspoon of lime butter inside each fish. Squeeze over the lime juice and sprinkle on seasoning. Fold the foil over the trout and seal. Steam for 15 minutes. Serve with remaining lime butter.

SERVES 2

SWORDFISH KEBABS

4 small white onions, peeled

½ pound swordfish or tuna fillets, cut in 1-inch squares

6 button mushrooms

½ red pepper, cut into pieces

MARINADE

1 tablespoon vegetable oil

pinch of thyme

pinch of marjoram

½ cup lemon juice

2 bay leaves

½ teaspoon chopped fresh parsley

Mix together the oil, thyme, marjoram, lemon juice, bay leaves and parsley.

Cut a cross in the root end of each onion to prevent the centers from falling out. Cook the onions whole in water for 15 minutes. Thread the fish squares on skewers alternately with the onions, mushrooms and pieces of pepper.

Put the fish kebabs in the marinade and leave for 1 hour, turning often. Broil for 10–15 minutes, turning frequently to cook all over. Alternatively, cook on a barbecue.

SERVES 2

DEEP-FRIED SCALLOPS AND SHRIMP

20 scallops

20 large shrimp

1 cup white wine

1 cup water

bouquet garni

freshly ground black pepper

whole wheat flour

oil for deep-frying

lime wedges

BATTER

1 cup whole wheat flour

1 cup milk

1 egg, separated

pinch of cayenne

TARTAR SAUCE

1 cup mayonnaise

1 teaspoon capers, finely chopped

1 teaspoon chopped chives

1 teaspoon Dijon mustard

To make the batter, sift the flour and blend in the milk, egg yolk and cayenne. Set aside to rest for 20 minutes. Beat the egg white until stiff and fold it into the batter.

To make the tartar sauce, whisk together the mayonnaise, capers, chives and mustard.

Clean the scallops. Peel and devein the shrimp. Bring the wine and water to a boil with the bouquet garni. Blanch the seafood in the liquid, remove and drain. Season the seafood, coat with flour and dip into batter. Deep-fry each piece until golden and drain. Serve hot with tartar sauce and lime wedges.

SERVES 4

Deep-fried Scallops and Shrimp (above) and Fish Florentine

BAKED CHICKEN ORIENTAL

2 pounds cut-up chicken

½ green pepper, cut in strips

½ red pepper, cut in strips

SAUCE

2 tablespoons cornstarch

¼ cup cider vinegar

1 tablespoon sugar

2 tablespoons chutney

1 teaspoon grated fresh ginger root

1 teaspoon soy sauce

1 cup pineapple pieces in natural juice

Preheat oven to 350°F. Place chicken in a baking dish large enough to fit. Mix together the cornstarch and vinegar in a small saucepan, add the sugar, chutney, ginger, soy and pineapple pieces, heat to boiling, and cook, stirring until thick. Pour the sauce over the chicken.

Bake 30 minutes, add the pepper strips and continue cooking an additional 15 minutes or until the chicken is done.

SERVES 4

CHICKEN FILLETS WITH TOMATO TOPPING

2 chicken breast fillets

1 tomato, chopped

½ small white onion, thinly sliced

1 teaspoon chopped fresh tarragon

½ teaspoon dried thyme

½ clove garlic, crushed

freshly ground black pepper

2 teaspoons butter, softened

Cut out two 12-inch squares of foil. Place one chicken fillet on each square.

Mix together the tomato, onion, tarragon, thyme, garlic, pepper and butter. Top each chicken fillet with the mixture. Fold the foil over the chicken and seal. Steam for 20 minutes and serve in the foil.

SERVES 2

FISH FLORENTINE

½ pound fish fillets

½ cup water

⅓ cup lemon juice

1 bay leaf

1 shallot, finely chopped

1 stalk celery, quartered

1 bunch or package of spinach, cooked

3 tablespoons grated Cheddar cheese

red pepper, to garnish

Put the fish into a pan and add the water, lemon juice, bay leaf, shallot and celery. Cover the pan and simmer for about 10 minutes or until the fish is tender.

Drain the spinach and arrange in the bottom of a casserole dish. Place the cooked fish over it, sprinkle with cheese and broil until the cheese has melted. Serve decorated with red pepper.

SERVES 2

SESAME GRILLED CHICKEN

2 skinned chicken fillets

2 tablespoons sesame seeds

MARINADE

½ carrot, chopped

½ onion, chopped

pinch of ground cloves

6 peppercorns

1 tablespoon chopped fresh parsley

½ teaspoon dried thyme

2 tablespoons vegetable oil

1 tablespoon lemon juice

¼ cup white wine

Mix together the marinade ingredients.

Arrange the chicken fillets on a flat dish and pour over the marinade. Let sit at least 1 hour.

Preheat the broiler to high. Place the chicken on foil, brush with the marinade and broil for 5 minutes. Turn and brush with more marinade and broil another 5 minutes or until the chicken is cooked. Turn off the broiler, brush the chicken with more

Sesame Grilled Chicken

marinade, shake sesame seeds over and leave under the turned-off broiler for a few minutes before serving. Slice fillets and serve with rice.

SERVES 2

VEAL PARMIGIANA

4 large veal scallops

freshly ground black pepper

1 cup flour, sifted

½ teaspoon dried oregano

2 eggs, beaten

½ cup grated Parmesan cheese

1½ cups prepared or fresh breadcrumbs

oil, for frying

1 cup grated mozzarella cheese

2 cups tomato sauce, fresh or canned

fresh oregano, to garnish

Preheat oven 350°F. Flatten the veal scallops with a meat mallet, season and coat with flour. Beat the oregano and eggs together in a shallow bowl. In a second bowl, combine the Parmesan with the breadcrumbs.

Dip each scallop into egg and coat with breadcrumbs. Heat the oil and fry each scallop over high heat for 1 minute on each side. Remove from the pan and place in a shallow casserole dish. Sprinkle each scallop with grated mozzarella and pour over the tomato sauce.

Bake for 10 minutes or until the cheese has melted. Serve garnished with oregano.

SERVES 4

SEAFOOD PASTA

24 mussels, well washed and debearded

1 cup dry white wine

½ pound sliced mushrooms

12 scallions, finely sliced

3½ tablespoons butter

1 pound large raw shrimp, peeled

bouquet garni

¼ teaspoon paprika

1 tablespoon brandy (optional)

½ pound pasta

¾ cup fresh or canned tomato purée

finely chopped fresh parsley

Put mussels in a large pot with the wine, cover the pan and cook over high heat until the shells open. Discard any that do not. Strain the liquid and reserve. Pick out a few of the best looking mussels for garnish; remove the meat from the others and set aside.

Cook the mushrooms and scallions in the butter for 3 minutes then add the shrimp, bouquet garni and paprika. Cook for a minute or two, add brandy if using, and flame. Douse the flames with the reserved mussel liquid and simmer for a few minutes more. Remove the shrimp and reduce the liquid in the pan by half.

Cook the pasta until tender and drain. Add tomato sauce to the mussel liquid and bring to the boil. Add mussels and shrimp and cook until just heated through. Discard bouquet garni. Put the pasta into a warmed serving plate, spoon the sauce over the top, decorate with reserved mussels in their shells and lots of chopped parsley.

SERVES 4–6

Seafood Pasta (above) and Veal Parmigiana

FISH PROVENÇALE

¾ pound firm fish fillets or steaks

⅓ cup lemon juice

freshly ground black pepper

1 clove garlic, crushed

2 tomatoes, peeled and sliced

¼ cup finely chopped fresh parsley

⅓ cup dry white wine

1 tablespoon chopped fresh basil

1 teaspoon **herbes de Provence**
*(dried thyme, rosemary,
marjoram and oregano)*

¼ cup pine nuts

Preheat broiler. Put the garlic,
tomatoes, parsley, wine and basil in
a saucepan, bring to the boil, reduce
heat and cook for 15 minutes.

Sprinkle fish with lemon juice and
pepper, and broil for 15 minutes
until fish is well cooked.

When tomato mixture has slightly
thickened, pour it over fish, sprinkle
on herbs and pine nuts, and serve.

SERVES 2

ORANGE CHICKEN PACKETS

2 skinned chicken fillets

1 tablespoon vegetable oil

1 small apple, thinly sliced

½ orange

orange zest, to garnish

scallions to garnish

Heat the oil in a medium skillet and
brown the chicken fillets. Cut out
two 12-inch squares of foil and place
a chicken fillet on each. Arrange
apple slices on top of the chicken
and squeeze orange juice over each.
Fold the foil over the fillets and seal.
Steam for 20 minutes. Serve in the
foil garnished with julienned orange
zest and scallions.

SERVES 2

FISH À LA GRECQUE

*2 large potatoes, peeled and
sliced*

1 onion, chopped

½ pound fish fillets

2 large tomatoes, sliced

½ cup water

2 tablespoons vegetable oil

freshly ground black pepper

½ cup finely chopped fresh parsley

Preheat oven to 300°F. Lay the
potato slices on the bottom of a
casserole dish and sprinkle with
chopped onion. Place fish fillets on
top and cover with sliced tomato.
Pour over the water and oil and
sprinkle with pepper and parsley.
Bake 30 minutes, or until fish flakes.

SERVES 2

TROUT IN FOIL

*2 small fresh trout, washed and
dried*

2 teaspoons butter

1 teaspoon lemon juice

1 teaspoon chopped fresh mint

Mix the butter with the lemon juice
and mint. Place half of this mixture
into the cavity of each trout.

Cut out two 12-inch squares of foil
and place a trout on each. Fold the
foil over the trout and seal. Steam
for 15 minutes. Serve in the foil
with lemon wedges.

SERVES 2

CURRIED CHICKEN

1 Granny Smith apple, peeled and sliced

1 onion, finely diced

1½ cups apple juice

2 tablespoons mango chutney

2 teaspoons curry powder

1 tablespoon flour

2 cups cooked chicken, cut into small pieces

1 banana, chopped

1 cup pineapple pieces

blanched almonds to garnish

Put the apple and onion into a saucepan with the apple juice and cook over low heat until the onion is soft. Add the mango chutney.

Blend the curry powder and flour together and make a paste with a little water. Add to the apple mixture and stir until thickened.

Just before serving, add the chicken pieces and heat through. Do not stir too much. Add the banana and pineapple pieces and serve garnished with blanched almonds. Serve with rice.

SERVES 4

GEFILTEFISH

1 pound whitefish fillets

1 egg, beaten

½ cup medium matzo meal

1 small onion, finely chopped

freshly ground black pepper

flour, for dusting

½ pound carrots, thinly sliced

2 cups fish stock

1 bay leaf

Preheat oven to 350°F. Mince or purée the fish and combine with the egg, matzo meal and onion and season to taste. Roll the mixture into 12 balls, using floured hands.

Arrange the carrots and fish balls in a shallow ovenproof dish, pour over the stock and add the bay leaf. Cover and bake for 1 hour. Remove the bay leaf before serving.

SERVES 4

BEEF COBBLER

1½ pounds stew beef, cut in pieces

¼ cup oil

1 onion, chopped

1 carrot, chopped

4 tablespoons flour

1 tablespoon tomato paste

1⅓ cups beef stock

1⅓ cups beer

1 clove garlic, crushed

pinch of dried rosemary

1 tablespoon milk

1 tablespoon chopped fresh parsley

Preheat oven to 300°F. Brown the meat in the oil, add the onion and carrot and cook for 5 minutes. Stir in the flour and cook for 1 minute. Add the remaining ingredients and bring to the boil.

Transfer to an ovenproof dish, cover and cook for 2 hours, or until the beef is tender.

SERVES 6

FISH IN FOIL PACKETS

2 teaspoons oil

4 fish fillets

½ teaspoon grated lemon rind

2 tablespoons lemon juice

2 tablespoons finely chopped parsley

1 teaspoon chopped fresh dill

1 tablespoon chopped fresh chives

freshly ground black pepper

½ teaspoon soy sauce

Cut out two 12-inch square pieces of foil and brush lightly with oil. Place 2 fish fillets on each square.

Mix together the lemon rind and juice, herbs, pepper and soy sauce. Spread the mixture over the fish pieces. Fold the foil over the fish and seal. Steam for 15 minutes. Serve in the foil.

SERVES 2

SPICY CHICKEN FILLETS

2 skinned chicken fillets

½ red pepper, cut into thin strips

½ green pepper, cut into thin strips

TOPPING

1 teaspoon grated fresh ginger root

½ clove garlic, crushed

½ cup mango chutney

pinch of cayenne

2 teaspoons butter, softened

Mix the topping ingredients together and set aside.

Cut out two 12-inch squares of foil and place a chicken fillet on each. Place topping mixture on the fillets and cover each with pepper strips.

Fold the foil over the chicken and seal. Steam for 20 minutes and serve in the foil.

SERVES 2

Accompaniments

*M*any of these vegetable dishes will also make fine first courses. Some, like Soufflé Potatoes, will make a light meal served with a salad. Most of the time you'll probably serve your vegetables simply boiled or steamed, but every now and again it's nice to give them a special lift by cooking them in a different way. This is especially true of potatoes, those most versatile of vegetables, so there are more potato dishes included than any other vegetable.

BROCCOLI IN CAPER SAUCE

1 pound broccoli

1 cup buttermilk

2 tablespoons cornstarch

1 cup yogurt

freshly ground black pepper

2 teaspoons chopped capers

½ teaspoon turmeric

4 tablespoons sour cream

Trim broccoli stalks and slit from base to flower. Peel the stalks if they look woody. Stand the stalks in boiling salted water with the flower heads above the water and cook for about 8 minutes, until the stalks are just tender. Drain and cover to keep warm while preparing the sauce.

Blend the buttermilk with the cornstarch and heat in a saucepan, stirring occasionally. Add the yogurt, pepper, capers and turmeric, stirring until the sauce thickens. Add the sour cream and heat through without boiling.

Place broccoli on a serving dish, spoon some sauce over and serve the remainder separately.

SERVES 4

SOUFFLÉ POTATOES

4 large old potatoes

1 cup grated Cheddar cheese

freshly ground black pepper

4 tablespoons sour cream

1 tablespoon chopped chives

1 tablespoon chopped fresh parsley

pinch of paprika

2 egg yolks

3 egg whites

Preheat oven to 350°F. Wash the potatoes, pierce with a skewer in several places and bake for 1–1½ hours. The potatoes should be cooked but still intact. Cut a lid off each potato and scoop out the center, leaving some of the flesh around the skin to form a casing.

Increase heat to 400°F. Mash the potato with all the remaining ingredients except the egg whites. Beat the egg whites until stiff and gently fold into the potato mixture. Spoon into potato cases and stand them up on an oven tray. Bake until the tops are golden brown and puffy.

SERVES 4

GLAZED ONIONS

18 small white onions, peeled

3 tablespoons butter

1 tablespoon olive oil

freshly ground black pepper

1 bay leaf

½ cup chicken stock

2 tablespoons white vermouth

2 tablespoons chopped fresh parsley

Preheat oven to 350°F. Cut a cross in the root end of each onion to prevent the centers from falling out. Brown them in butter and oil. Season with pepper.

Place onions with their cooking butter into a baking dish. Add bay leaf, chicken stock and vermouth.

Cover and bake 1 hour. Turn onions every 20 minutes. Garnish with parsley to serve.

SERVES 6

DHAL

1 pound lentils

1–2 tablespoons ghee or oil

2–3 onions, finely sliced

2–3 tomatoes, peeled and chopped

1 teaspoon chili powder

2 teaspoons turmeric

salt

2 tablespoons tomato paste

Soak the lentils in water to cover for 30 minutes. Heat the ghee and sauté the onions until they are soft but not brown. Add tomatoes, chili powder, turmeric and salt. Cook, stirring, for 5 minutes.

Drain the lentils and put them in a pan with enough water to cover. Bring to the boil, add the onion mixture and simmer for 1 hour until thick and mushy. Stir in tomato paste and serve with rice or curried vegetables.

SERVES 8

POTATO CROQUETTES

1 tablespoon milk

1½ tablespoons butter

2 egg yolks

1 pound potatoes, cooked and mashed

freshly ground black pepper

1 tablespoon chopped fresh parsley

1 egg, beaten

breadcrumbs

oil, for deep-frying

Heat the milk in a pan and add the butter. Off heat, stir until the butter has melted. Stir in egg yolks. Beat in mashed potatoes, pepper and parsley. Divide into portions and shape into croquettes.

Dip in beaten egg and roll in breadcrumbs. Deep-fry in hot oil until brown. Drain on paper before serving. The croquettes may be kept warm in a low oven or made beforehand and reheated.

SERVES 4–6

BAKED TURNIPS

2 turnips, peeled and diced

½ cup chicken stock

4 tablespoons dark honey

Preheat the oven to 350°F. Put turnips in a buttered casserole dish. Mix warm stock with honey and pour over the turnips. Cover and bake for 45 minutes or until tender.

SERVES 4

Previous pages: Clockwise from top left: Fennel Sauté, Orange Glazed Carrots, Braised Broad Beans, Baby Squash with Dill, Glazed Brussels Sprouts and Parsnips with Herbs

FENNEL SAUTÉ

3 fennel bulbs

4 tablespoons butter

freshly ground black pepper

grated peel of ½ lemon

juice of ½ lemon

1 tablespoon chopped fresh parsley

fresh chives, to garnish

Wash fennel and cut into thin slices from top to bottom. Melt the butter in a pan, add the fennel, cover and cook for 5 minutes. Remove the lid and cook for a further 5 minutes. Transfer to a serving dish and keep it warm.

Add the remaining ingredients to the pan, heat through and pour over the fennel. Serve garnished with chives.

SERVES 4

PARSNIPS WITH HERBS

6 parsnips

6 tablespoons butter

juice 1 lemon

freshly ground black pepper

1 cup chicken stock

1 tablespoon finely chopped fresh herbs (parsley, chives, dill, marjoram)

fresh thyme, for decoration

Peel parsnips and cut into large matchsticks. Put the butter, lemon juice, pepper and stock into a skillet and bring to the boil. Add the parsnips and herbs and cook, uncovered, until the stock has reduced and the parsnips are tender. Add more stock if necessary. Garnish with thyme.

SERVES 4

BABY SQUASH WITH DILL

1 pound miniature squash, trimmed

4 tablespoons butter

1 cup water

freshly ground black pepper

1 tablespoon finely chopped fresh dill

juice ½ lemon

fresh dill, to garnish

Place squash in a heavy saucepan with butter and water. Season with pepper. Cover the pan and bring to the boil, reduce heat and simmer for 5 minutes.

Add dill and lemon juice, and boil, uncovered, until the liquid has almost evaporated. Serve immediately garnished with dill.

SERVES 4–6

ORANGE GLAZED CARROTS

¼ pound (1 stick) butter

juice of 2 oranges

¼ cup brown sugar

1 pound carrots, cut into sticks

¼ teaspoon cinnamon

fresh basil, to garnish

Melt the butter in a deep saucepan. Stir in the orange juice and sugar and bring to the boil. Lower the heat and cook for 3 minutes, stirring constantly.

Add the carrots, sprinkle with cinnamon and cook, stirring from time to time, until the juice has almost evaporated and the carrots are tender. Decorate with basil.

SERVES 6

GLAZED BRUSSELS SPROUTS

2 pounds Brussels sprouts
1½ cups chicken stock
10 tablespoons honey
pinch of ground cloves
1 tablespoon lemon juice
fresh sage, to garnish

Trim the Brussels sprouts, cut the stalks level with the base and cut a cross into the base. Bring a pot of water to the boil and blanch the sprouts briefly.

Drain and place in a heavy saucepan. Barely cover with chicken stock and add honey and cloves. Cook until just tender. Remove sprouts and keep warm while reducing liquid by boiling briskly. When liquid has halved in quantity, add lemon juice, pour mixture over sprouts and serve garnished with sage.

SERVES 6–8

POTATO STICKS

½ pound potatoes
2 egg yolks
4 tablespoons butter
1¼ cups flour
freshly ground black pepper
1 tablespoon chopped chives
1 egg, beaten

Preheat oven to 400°F. Peel the potatoes and cook in boiling salted water until tender. Drain and mash with the egg yolks and butter until creamy. Add the flour, pepper and chives and mix well. Form the dough into a round shape and chill for 30 minutes.

Roll potatoes out into a rectangle ½ inch thick. Cut into sticks ½ inch wide and 2½ inches long. Twist and brush lightly with beaten egg.

Place on a greased oven tray and bake for 10 minutes or until golden brown and crisp. Leave on the tray until cool.

MAKES 40

Baked Turnips (left) and Potato Sticks

BABY CARROTS
WITH FRESH BASIL

....

*1 pound baby carrots, well
   scrubbed*

*2 tablespoons finely chopped fresh
   basil*

3 tablespoons butter

Place carrots in a saucepan and just
cover with boiling water. Cover the
pan, bring to the boil and cook for
10 minutes. Drain, toss well with
basil, add butter and return to the
heat. Allow the butter to melt,
mixing well with the carrots.

SERVES 6

Baby Carrots with Fresh Basil

SWEDISH HASSELBACK POTATOES

12 potatoes, peeled

1 teaspoon salt

4 tablespoons butter

4 tablespoons grated Parmesan cheese

2 tablespoons breadcrumbs

Preheat oven to 450°F. Cut potatoes into thin slices but not quite through to the lower edge, so that the slices hold together.

Place potatoes, with slices up, into a well-buttered casserole. Sprinkle with salt and dot with butter. Bake for 20 minutes, basting occasionally with the melted butter. Sprinkle with cheese and breadcrumbs and bake for another 25 minutes without basting.

SERVES 6

BRAISED BROAD BEANS

2 pounds fresh broad beans in their pods (2 cups shelled)

4 tablespoons oil

1 onion, chopped

1 clove garlic, crushed

1 tablespoon chopped fresh parsley

1 tablespoon chopped fresh dill

freshly ground black pepper

pinch of nutmeg

1½ cups water mixed with 1½ tablespoons tomato purée

Shell beans. Heat the oil in a saucepan, add the beans, onion and garlic and cook over moderate heat, stirring, for 2 minutes. Add the remaining ingredients and bring to the boil.

Add enough water to keep the mixture from frying and cover the pan. Cook for 25 minutes, adding more water if necessary.

SERVES 6

SWEET POTATOES WITH PINEAPPLE IN FOIL

1 large sweet potato, peeled and sliced in ½-inch thick slices

4 tablespoons pineapple, chopped

2 teaspoons margarine

ORANGE AND GINGER SAUCE

2 tablespoons cornstarch

1 cup orange juice

1 tablespoon margarine

1 teaspoon orange rind, grated

½ teaspoon ground ginger

Cut out 2 sheets of foil about 12 inches square. Place half the potato slices on each piece of foil and top with pineapple and margarine. Fold the foil over the sweet potatoes and seal. Steam for 20 minutes. Serve with sauce.

To make sauce, in a pan blend cornstarch with a little orange juice. Add remaining juice, margarine, grated orange rind and ginger, and thicken over gentle heat.

SERVES 2

RATATOUILLE

½ small eggplant, sliced and cut into quarters

1 zucchini, sliced

1 carrot, sliced

¼ red pepper, sliced

¼ green pepper, sliced

1 onion, peeled and sliced

1 clove garlic, finely chopped

3 tomatoes, roughly chopped

1 tablespoon chopped fresh basil

Place all ingredients in a non-stick frying pan and cook gently for 30 minutes. Stir from time to time to prevent sticking.

SERVES 2

MEXICAN SUCCOTASH

½ red pepper, cut into ¾-inch squares

½ green pepper, cut into ¾-inch squares

4 small white onions, halved

½ cup fresh shelled peas

½ cup fresh corn kernels

½ cup fresh lima beans

1 tablespoon oil

1 tablespoon chopped fresh basil

fresh basil or parsley, to garnish

Place all the vegetables in a steamer and cook for 10 minutes.

In a pan, heat oil and stir vegetables around for several minutes. Add basil and serve with fresh herbs.

SERVES 2

STRING BEANS WITH ALMONDS

1 pound string beans, sliced

4 tablespoons toasted, slivered almonds

butter, to serve

Place beans and almonds in a steamer. Cover and steam for 6 minutes. Top with butter and serve in a hot dish.

SERVES 4

Fruit and Desserts

*T*he healthiest and usually the most delicious dessert is fresh fruit in season. Strawberries in spring and late summer, summer peaches and plums, apples and pears in the fall, varieties of citrus in winter, and tropical fruit almost all year round. There's a chart on pages 18–19 showing some of the new tropical fruit available and how to prepare and eat it.

However, sometimes we all have a craving for dessert. In winter especially, a dried fruit crumble or a rice dish is comforting and warming. And when at the end of the season we've had enough of fresh strawberries, a strawberry sorbet makes a delicious change. Most of the recipes here are based on fruit and they're all very simple to prepare.

POACHED PEACHES

4 fresh peaches

¼ cup flaked coconut

¼ cup ground almonds

½ teaspoon finely grated orange rind

1 egg yolk

3 tablespoons butter

1 cup white wine

1 cinnamon stick

Blanch peaches in boiling water and leave for 1 minute. Drain, cover with cold water and peel. Slice the peaches and remove the pits. Arrange slices in a baking dish. Preheat oven to 350°F.

Mix together the coconut, almonds, orange rind and egg yolk and spoon it between the peach slices. Dot with butter, pour wine around the peaches and add the cinnamon stick. Cover and bake for 20 minutes or until the peaches are tender. Remove the cinnamon stick and serve warm with custard.

SERVES 4

KISSEL

2 cups blackberries

juice of 1 lemon

¼ cup honey

⅛ teaspoon powdered cinnamon

2 cups water

1½ tablespoons arrowroot

1½ tablespoons potato flour

⅔ cup yogurt or sour cream

Put blackberries, lemon juice, honey, and cinnamon in a pan with 1¼ cups water and bring to a boil. Cook 5 minutes. Strain through sieve or purée in blender. Return mixture to pan and bring back to boil.

Mix arrowroot and potato flour with remaining water and add to blackberry purée. Cook 4 minutes then pour into individual dishes and cool. Serve topped with yogurt or sour cream.

SERVES 4

GINGER SOUFFLÉ

4 tablespoons butter

3 tablespoons flour

1½ cups milk

2 tablespoons sugar

3 eggs, separated

1 teaspoon vanilla extract

2 teaspoons grated ginger in syrup

confectioner's sugar, sieved

Preheat oven to 375°F. Melt the butter in a saucepan, stir in the flour and cook for 1 minute. Add the milk gradually, stirring constantly, to form a smooth sauce. Add the sugar and stir until it has dissolved. Cool the sauce slightly.

Beat the egg yolks into the sauce with the vanilla essence and ginger. Beat the egg whites until stiff and fold them into the sauce. Spoon the mixture into a soufflé dish and bake for 40 minutes or until puffed and golden, and a skewer inserted in the side comes out clean. Sprinkle with confectioner's sugar and serve immediately.

SERVES 4-6

DRIED FRUIT CRUMBLE

1 cup dried apricots

1 cup dried figs

1 cup pitted prunes

¼ cup raisins

¼ cup currants

¼ cup sugar

1 cup water

¼ cup almonds

2 tablespoons flour

¼ cup desiccated coconut

¼ cup brown sugar

3 tablespoons butter

Soak the fruit for 1 hour in enough water to cover, then drain. Place the sugar and water in a saucepan and bring to the boil. Add the fruit and simmer for 30 minutes or until the liquid has been absorbed. Add the almonds and place the mixture in an ovenproof serving dish.

Preheat oven to 400°F. Combine the flour, coconut, sugar and butter and sprinkle over the fruit. Bake for 15–20 minutes or until the top is golden.

SERVES 4-6

PINEAPPLE CALYPSO

1 ripe pineapple

6 tablespoons chopped fresh mint

2 egg whites

½ cup superfine sugar

Peel the pineapple and cut it into quarters lengthwise. Remove the hard core from the center of each quarter and cut the pineapple into small cubes. Mix with the chopped mint and chill overnight. Preheat broiler.

Spoon the pineapple into ramekins or custard cups. Beat the egg whites until soft peaks are formed and add half the sugar. Continue to beat, adding remaining sugar, until whites are stiff. Spoon over the pineapple. Place under a broiler to brown the meringue.

SERVES 4

APRICOT MOUSSE

1 pound ripe apricots

juice of ½ lemon

3 tablespoons confectioner's sugar

2 teaspoons gelatin

¼ cup cold water

½ cup heavy cream

whipped cream (optional)

mint leaves, to garnish

Blanch apricots in boiling water and leave for 1 minute. Drain, cover with cold water and peel. Cut the apricots in half and remove pits. Purée the apricots with lemon juice and confectioner's sugar in a blender or rub through a sieve.

Sprinkle gelatin into the water and stand over a bowl of hot water until dissolved. Stir it into the apricot purée.

Beat the cream until stiff and fold into the apricot mixture. Spoon into individual serving dishes and chill until set. Serve with whipped cream garnished with mint leaves.

SERVES 4

CHINESE PEARS

4 ripe pears

1 quart water

½ cup sugar

1 cinnamon stick

4 cloves

3 tablespoons chopped walnuts

3 tablespoons chopped dates

¼ cup honey

2 teaspoons ground ginger

1 tablespoon lemon juice

lemon peel cut in strips

toasted slivered almonds

Above: Chinese Pears
Left: Apricot Mousse

Peel the pears, cut them in half lengthwise and remove the core, or use whole, as desired. Place pears in a baking dish, cut side up. Cover with water, add sugar, cinnamon and cloves and poach until tender.

In a saucepan, mix together walnuts, dates, honey, ginger, lemon juice and peel. Add a little water and heat gently.

Serve pears with sauce, garnished with almonds.

SERVES 4

FRUIT BRÛLÉE

4 cups prepared fruit

1 cup cream

4 tablespoons brown sugar

¼ teaspoon cinnamon

SPUN CARAMEL

½ cup sugar

water

Use any fruit in season for this dessert; seedless grapes, peeled and seeded; cherries, pitted; apricots, pitted and quartered; strawberries, hulled; kiwifruit, peeled and sliced. Place fruit in 4 individual ovenproof serving dishes and pour ¼ cup cream into each. Chill overnight.

Just before serving, sprinkle 1 tablespoon brown sugar and a little cinnamon over each and place under the broiler until the sugar melts and browns. Garnish with spun caramel.

To make spun caramel, heat sugar in a saucepan. Brush edges of pan with water using a pastry brush to dissolve crystals. Stir until sugar is dissolved. When caramel is boiling do not stir. Heat gently until a golden brown. It should be tacky when two spoons are touched together. Remove from the heat and spin caramel using spoons. Cut strands with scissors and arrange on top of fruit.

SERVES 4

ALMOND BANANA CREAM

2 bananas, peeled and sliced

2 teaspoons honey

½ cup ground almonds

6 strawberries

Wrap the banana slices in foil and freeze for 4 to 5 hours. Remove from the freezer and let stand for 5 minutes.

Put them in a blender with the honey, almonds and strawberries. Blend until they are puréed and serve immediately.

SERVES 2

Fruit Brûlée

APPLE CRUMBLE

3 apples, peeled, cored and sliced

1 cup orange juice

CRUMBLE

2 teaspoons butter

½ cup rolled oats

½ cup chopped almonds

2 teaspoons brown sugar

1 teaspoon ground cinnamon

Put the apples in a pan with the orange juice and cook over low heat for 15 minutes. Place into a cake pan or deep pie dish. Preheat oven to 350°F.

To make the crumble, melt the butter in a saucepan and add the oats, almonds, sugar and cinnamon.

Sprinkle the crumble on top of the stewed apples and bake for 20 minutes or until the topping is brown.

SERVES 2

APRICOT AND NUT TART

PASTRY

1 cup flour

2 tablespoons chopped almonds

2 tablespoons chopped walnuts

1 tablespoon sugar

3 tablespoons butter

1 egg

2 tablespoons lemon juice

iced water

FILLING

One large (15-ounce) can apricot halves

2 tablespoons chopped dried apricots

4 tablespoons chopped almonds

1 egg yolk

2 egg whites

4 tablespoons sugar

extra apricot halves for decoration (optional)

To make the pastry, place the flour, nuts and sugar in a bowl and rub in the butter with your fingertips. Mix together the egg and lemon juice and add to the flour mixture with enough iced water to form a firm dough. Wrap in plastic and chill for 20 minutes. Roll out the dough to fit an 8 to 9-inch quiche pan. Chill while you prepare the filling. Preheat oven to 350°F.

Drain the apricots and purée them in a blender or strain through a sieve. Mix in the dried apricots, almonds and egg yolk. Beat the egg whites until stiff, add sugar and beat until it has dissolved. Fold into the apricot mixture and spoon into the pastry-lined quiche pan. Bake for 1 hour. Decorate with extra apricot halves if desired.

SERVES 6

RAINBOW RICE PUDDING

½ cup chopped pitted prunes

½ cup chopped dried apricots

½ cup chopped raisins

1 cup boiling water

juice ½ lemon

1 cup cooked brown rice

½ teaspoon nutmeg

½ teaspoon cinnamon

2 egg yolks

1 cup milk

Pour boiling water over fruit and let stand 1 hour. Drain and stir in the lemon juice. Mix the rice with the nutmeg, cinnamon, egg yolks and milk. Preheat the oven to 325°F.

Starting and finishing with a rice layer, put alternate layers of fruit and rice in a well-greased soufflé

dish. Cover the dish and bake for 1 hour.

Remove from the oven and stand the dish in a pan of warm water for 10 minutes. Run a knife around the edge, and turn the pudding out onto a serving dish. Serve hot or cold.

SERVES 4–6

TROPICAL SHERBET

1 cup fresh pineapple pieces

1 cup papaya or mango pieces

1 banana, chopped

½ cup orange juice

2 passion fruit

2 teaspoons honey

Place all the ingredients in a blender and blend until smooth. Pour into an ice cream tray and freeze. Return the frozen mixture to the blender and blend again, just until it has a sorbet texture. If you blend too long, it will liquify. Serve immediately, before it has time to thaw.

SERVES 3

PEAR SHERBET

½ cup apple juice

2 pears, peeled and sliced

1 cup seedless grapes

1 cup peeled apple pieces

4 dates, pitted

1 cup strawberries

Place all ingredients in a blender and process until smooth. Pour into an ice cream tray and freeze. Return the frozen fruit to the blender and blend carefully until it reaches the texture of sorbet. Serve immediately.

SERVES 4

PUMPKIN PIE

PASTRY

> 1 cup self-rising flour
> 1 cup whole wheat flour
> ¼ pound (1 stick) butter
> 1 egg yolk
> 2 tablespoons lemon juice
> iced water

FILLING

> 1 cup cooked pumpkin
> 1 tablespoon brown sugar
> 2 eggs, separated
> 4 tablespoons cream
> ¼ teaspoon nutmeg
> ¼ teaspoon ground ginger

To make the pastry, place the flours in a bowl and rub in the butter with your fingertips. Mix the egg yolk with the lemon juice, add to the flour mixture with enough iced water to make a smooth dough. Form into a ball, wrap in plastic and chill for 20 minutes. Roll out the dough, line an 8-inch pie dish and set aside in the refrigerator for 20 minutes.

Preheat oven to 350°F. Place the pumpkin in a blender or food processor with the sugar, egg yolks, cream, nutmeg and ginger. Blend to a purée. Beat the egg whites until stiff and fold into the pumpkin mixture. Pour into the pastry-lined pie dish and bake for 35 minutes or until the pastry is golden and the filling has set. Serve warm.

SERVES 6

ORANGE AND RHUBARB COMPOTE

> 1 bunch rhubarb
> 2 oranges
> ½ cup brown sugar
> ¼ cup water

Preheat oven to 350°F. Wash the rhubarb and trim the stalks. Cut into 1½-inch lengths. Peel the oranges, making sure all the pith is removed. Cut into thin rounds and remove all pips.

Layer the fruit in a baking dish and sprinkle with sugar. Add water and bake at until the rhubarb is tender. Serve hot or cold.

SERVES 4

BAKED APPLE AND TAPIOCA PUDDING

> 2¾ cups milk
> ¼ cup tapioca
> 3 eggs
> 2 tablespoons honey
> ⅛ teaspoon ground nutmeg
> ⅛ teaspoon ground cloves
> 2 apples peeled, cored and sliced
> 3 tablespoons butter

Preheat oven to 350°F. Bring milk and tapioca to boil and cook 8 minutes. Leave to cool. Beat in eggs, honey and spices. Gently cook apples in butter until soft. Arrange in soufflé dish and fill dish with tapioca mixture. Place dish in baking tray half filled with hot water and bake for 45 minutes. Serve cold.

SERVES 4

PEAR AND DATE CRUNCH

> 1½ pounds pears, peeled and cored
> ½ pound dates, halved and pitted
> 1 tablespoon raw sugar
> ½ teaspoon ground allspice
> ⅔ cup orange juice

TOPPING

> ¼ pound (1 stick) butter
> 1¼ cups whole wheat flour
> ¼ cup raw or brown sugar
> ½ cup rolled oats
> ½ teaspoon cinnamon

Preheat oven to 350°F. Cut pears into chunky pieces and place in ovenproof dish with dates, sugar, allspice and orange juice.

Rub butter into flour, stir in sugar, oats and cinnamon. Sprinkle over fruit. Bake for 40 minutes or until pears are soft and topping golden. Serve hot.

SERVES 6

MACERATED FRUITS

> 4 to 5 pounds summer fruit (pears, plums, strawberries, raspberries, cherries, apricots, bananas and peaches)
> lemon juice
> 2 tablespoons honey
> 2½-3 cups rosé wine
> yogurt or cream, to serve

Prepare fruit and slice or halve according to size. Sprinkle lemon juice over any likely to brown (such as apples, pears or bananas). Layer fruit in large serving dish.

Stir honey into wine and pour over fruit. Leave overnight in refrigerator. Serve with yogurt or cream.

SERVES 6-8

STRAWBERRY SORBET

1 pint strawberries

1 cup water

¼ cup sugar

½ cup ice cream

2 tablespoons lemon juice

2 tablespoons Kirsch

2 egg whites

¼ cup superfine sugar

extra whole strawberries, to garnish

Wash and hull the strawberries. Place them in a blender with the water, sugar, ice cream, lemon juice and Kirsch and purée. Pour the mixture into 2 ice trays and freeze.

Beat the egg whites until stiff, add the superfine sugar and beat until dissolved. Remove the strawberry ice from the freezer and break up with a fork. Fold the egg whites into the strawberry mixture and spoon into individual serving bowls. Freeze, stirring every 10 minutes until the mixture is firm. When serving, decorate with strawberries.

SERVES 4

STEAMED APPLES IN FOIL

2 apples, cored and stuffed with dates or raisins

½ teaspoon honey or maple syrup

Cut out two 12-inch squares of foil. Place an apple on each and drizzle with honey. Fold the foil over the apples and seal. Steam for 15 minutes. Serve hot.

SERVES 2

Strawberry Sorbet

Menus

LUNCH AND LIGHT MEALS

Potato Soufflé
Mixed Salad
Fruit and Cheese

....

Cheesy Carrot Ring
Mixed Green Salad
Fruit

....

Chilled Pumpkin Soup
Farmhouse Salad

....

Eggplant and Walnut Puff
Green Salad

....

Vegetable Strudel
Mixed Green Salad

....

Spanakopita
Fresh Fruit

....

Vegetable Pâté
Beef Cobbler
Green Salad

....

Vegetable Kebabs
Boiled Brown Rice
Chinese Pears

....

Potatoes Czarina
Green Salad
Fruit

....

Stuffed Artichokes
Apricot and Nut Tart

....

Seafood Pasta
Green Salad
Fruit

....

Iced Orange and Tomato Soup
Sesame Grilled Chicken
Mixed Salad

....

PARTY FOOD

Raw vegetables, cut into strips and
served with
Broad Bean Pâté
Eggplant Purée
Shrimp Pâté

....

Hot Cheese Balls

....

Rice Croquettes with Tomato Sauce

....

Shrimp Rascals

....

Potato Sticks

....

SLIMMING MENUS

Tomatoes Granita
Tofu Spinach Soufflé
Fresh Fruit

....

Russian Red Cabbage Salad
Gefiltefish

....

Iced Buttermilk Soup
Mixed Salad

....

Lemon Soup
Fresh Fruit

....

Fish Florentine
Fresh Fruit

....

Fish in Foil Packets
Mixed Salad
Fresh Fruit

....

RELAXED SUMMER DINNERS

Tomatoes Roquefort
Herbed Jellied Meat Loaf
Spicy Bean Sprouts

....

Iced Orange and Tomato Soup
Veal Parmigiana
Apricot Mousse

....

Cream of Chayote Soup
Lamb and Nut Korma
Strawberry Sorbet

....

Iced Beet Soup
Broad Bean Casserole
Fruit Brûlée

....

Trout in Foil
Herbed Green Beans
Poached Peaches

....

Orange Chicken Packets
Mixed Salad
Fruit Brûlée

....

Steamed Trout in Lime Butter
Green Salad
Fresh Fruit

....

Spicy Chicken Fillets
Brown Rice
Green Salad
Fresh Fruit

....

Grilled Marinated Fish
Tropical Sherbet

....

Vegetable Pâté
Swordfish Kebabs

....

Fish Provençale
Steamed Apples in Foil

....

Chicken Hawaiian
Apricot Mousse

....

Clockwise from top: Fresh fruit and cheese, Broiled Kingfish Steaks, Green Salad and Spanakopita

WINTER MENUS

Minestrone
Green Salad
Rainbow Rice Pudding

Stuffed Turnips
Apollo Steak
Glazed Brussels Sprouts
Ginger Soufflé

Grilled Mushroom Caps
Eggplant Khoresh
Orange and Rhubarb Compote

Bean and Pea Soup
Green Salad
Pumpkin Pie

Cashew Nut Roast
Green Salad
Dried Fruit Crumble

Barley Vegetable Casserole
Green Salad

Fish Pie
Pear Sherbet

Baked Fish Casserole
Apple Crumble

Chicken Chasseur
Almond Banana Cream

LIGHT FAMILY MEALS

Fresh Tomato Soup
Zucchini and Cheese Salad
Fresh Fruit

Mughal Vegetables
Boiled Brown Rice
Pumpkin Pie

Curried Fish Risotto
Green Salad

Deep-fried Scallops and Shrimp
Green Salad
Fresh Fruit

Spanish Omelet
Farmhouse Salad
Apricot Mousse

Baked Vegetable Ring with Tomato Filling
Green Salad
Fresh Fruit

Watercress and Vermicelli Soup
Green Salad
Fruit and Cheese

Carrot and Orange Soup
Potato Soufflé
Green Salad

Spanish-style Sardines
Vegetable Kebabs

Macaroni and Zucchini Salad
Spicy Peanut Roast Chicken

Chilled Green Pea Soup
Fish with Peanut Sauce

Spinach Tarts
Mixed Salad

Stir-fry Tofu
Mixed Salad
Fresh Fruit

Fish à la Grecque
Green Salad
Strawberry Sorbet

Curried Chicken
Brown Rice
Fresh Fruit

Baked Oriental Chicken
Orange and Rhubarb Compote

Chicken Fillets with Tomato Topping
Apricot Mousse

High-fiber Menus

Bean Salad
Fresh Fruit

Orange and Spinach Salad
Ribbon Bean Bake

Curried Brown Rice Salad
Provençale Chicken
Country Harvest Soup
Green Salad

Lentil Soup
Green Salad
Fresh Fruit

Braised Chinese Vegetables
Hungarian Bean and Vegetable Loaf

Menus for Fitness

Fruit and Nut Salad
Pumpkin Pie

Tropical Rice Salad
Fresh Fruit

Lemon Soup
Zyldyk Casserole

Stir-fried Chicken
Mixed Salad

Cabbage Cake
Green Salad

Bean and Vegetable Tacos
Fruit

Minestrone
Green Salad

Chinese Green Soup
Poached Peaches

Crunchy Nut Terrine
Green Salad

Hot Rice Salad
Apricot and Nut Tart

Quick Meals

Instant Bean Medley
Green Salad

Melon Ambrosia

Gazpacho on Ice
Orange and Avocado Salad

Cold Yogurt and Cucumber Soup
Broiled Kingfish Steaks

Left to right: Watercress and Vermicelli Soup, Sesame Grilled Chicken, Green Salad and Poached Peaches

Index